JOHN OF THE CROSS

Man and Mystic

By

Richard P. Hardy

Pauline
BOOKS & MEDIA
Boston

Library of Congress Cataloging-in-Publication Data

Hardy, Richard P.
   John of the Cross : man and mystic / by Richard P. Hardy.
      p. cm.
   Includes bibliographical references.
   ISBN 0-8198-3980-9 (pbk.)
   1. John of the Cross, Saint, 1542-1591. 2. Christian saints—
Spain—Biography.
   I. Title.
   BX4700.J7H365 2004
   271'.7302—dc22
   [B]

                            2003027199

Cover art: Sr. Marie Celeste Fadden, o.c.d. (Carmel of Our Lady of the Mountains, 1950 La Fond Drive, Reno, Nevada 89509-3099)

"P" and PAULINE are registered trademarks of the Daughters of Saint Paul

Printed and published in the U.S.A. by Pauline Books & Media, 50 Saint Paul's Avenue, Boston, MA 02130-3491.

www.pauline.org

Pauline Books & Media is the publishing house of the Daughters of Saint Paul, an international congregation of women religious serving the Church with the communications media.

1 2 3 4 5 6 7 8 9   11 10 09 08 07 06 05 04

To the women and men of the
Discalced Carmelite Order throughout the world,
in thanks for their lives of enfleshing
the Spirit of John of the Cross and
Teresa of Avila in our time.

Contents

ACKNOWLEDGMENTS

I gratefully acknowledge permission for quotations from:

The Collected Works of St. John of the Cross, translated by Kieran Kavanaugh, O.C.D. and Otilio Rodriguez, O.C.D., with Revisions and Introductions by Kieran Kavanaugh, O.C.D. Copyright © 1991 by the Washington Province of Discalced Carmelite Friars, Inc., ICS Publications, 2131 Lincoln Road, N.E. Washington, D.C., 20002-1199, U.S.A. www.icspublications.org

The Collected Works of St. Teresa of Avila, Volume Three, translated by Kieran Kavanaugh, O.C.D. and Otilio Rodriguez, O.C.D. Copyright © 1980 by Washington Province of Discalced Carmelites, Inc., ICS Publications, 2131 Lincoln Road, N.E. Washington, D.C., 20002-1199, U.S.A. www.icspublications.org

The Collected Letters of St. Teresa of Avila, Volume One, translated by Kieran Kavanaugh, O.C.D. Copyright © 2001 by Washington Province of Discalced Carmelites, Inc., ICS Publications, 2131 Lincoln Road, N.E., Washington, D.C., 20002-1199, U.S.A. www.icspublications.org

INTRODUCTION

Since *Search for Nothing: The Life of John of the Cross*[1] went out of print, many people, including Carmelite scholars, religious, and lay women and men, have asked me if I would publish it again. While such support encouraged me, it did not seem possible at the time. However, while I was teaching a course on Fray Juan de la Cruz at Saint Michael's College in Vermont, the possibility did arise. This time, Sr. Madonna Ratliff of the Daughters of St. Paul in Boston asked if I might consider publishing a revised and updated version of the book. After talking with several people who very strongly suggested I should do it, I contacted Sr. Ratliff and accepted her suggestion to update and revise my original work. This book is the result of that decision.

When I began studying the works of Fray Juan de la Cruz over thirty years ago, I had been ill at ease with most of the biographies written about him. Though I was impressed by Jean Baruzi's biographical section in his classic work, *Saint Jean de la Croix et le problème de l'expérience mystique,*[2] other works in the same vein did not quite reach this stature. Even the scholarly work by Crisogono de Jesús and that by Bruno de Jésus-Marie,[3] as well as the more popular biographies published in the nineteenth or early part of the twentieth century, did not seem to really grasp Fray Juan de la Cruz the man. Although these authors had worked with the manuscripts concerning his canonization and had attempted to be faithful to the witnesses of his time, they continued a tradition of hagiography. In fact, they created a saint in their own image of the meaning of sanctity, and that is understandable.

Each age paints a picture of people that corresponds to its time and worldview. This is especially true when it concerns those extraordinary Christians whom we call saints. Thus, these biographers of Fray Juan portrayed a dismal, dark personality who seemed bent upon escaping this world and entering the next. Their Juan de la Cruz was a paragon of virtue and strength. According to them, miracles and heavenly hosts always protected him from evil. These authors seemed to delight in vying with each other in presenting some atrocious practices in which Fray Juan was supposed to have engaged in the name of asceticism and mysticism. The result is a portrait of someone who seems hardly human. As presented by them, Fray Juan is not a man anyone of our own century could imitate, and they do not inspire much desire to imitate him. However, even these authors and the witnesses upon whom they depend could not help seeing in Fray Juan some very human qualities: his sense of humor, his love for his family, his deep love of beauty, his concern for his neighbor, and his love of delightful things. But his contemporaries and most of his biographers did not view these qualities as the stuff of a saint. Consequently, these characteristics were either forgotten or hidden, remaining lost in what people of sixteenth-century Spain would consider the life of a true saint.

For me, these biographies did not reveal the true Fray Juan de la Cruz, the man I had come to know in reading his *Spiritual Canticle* or his *Living Flame of Love*. They did not adequately reflect the author of the sensual, world-loving *Romances on Creation*. They did not really help me to understand his counsels to religious about detachment or to penetrate the meaning of his *The Ascent of Mount Carmel* or *The Dark Night of the Soul*. After reading these works and biographies, I would ask myself, "Was Fray Juan indeed such a paradox? Are we to admit that his life and his works simply were too disparate and should always be kept apart?" Somehow, I could not answer yes to these questions.

The more I read and reread his works, the more I found that they spoke of a man so different from the one I had read about in biographies. So, I set out to do something about it. I determined to research his life once more. I went to Rome and worked in the Vatican Secret Archives, which hold some of the canonization and beatification documents, invaluable sources for a biographer of Fray Juan. In the same city, I was able to work in the library of the Teresianum, which has some of the earliest biographies of Fray Juan. Here Padre Eulogio Pacho, O.C.D. and his team of Discalced Carmelite researchers and scholars helped me greatly. They introduced me to the Calced Carmelites, who also let me use their library facilities. I then traveled throughout Spain, seeing the places Fray Juan himself had seen and where he lived. There I worked on early documents, which are to be found in the Discalced Carmelite monastery in Ubeda, where Fray Juan died, and in the Biblioteca Nacional de Madrid, whose staff very eagerly assisted me.

Slowly a new figure emerged: a man, a human being who had fallen in love with God IN the world. I discovered a man who is indeed a saint, but not because he fled the world. I found a man who had discovered that sanctity meant searching for and finding God in THIS world of ours and in the vicissitudes of his own life and times. Here was a man for whom the incarnation of the Word of God in Jesus meant the consecration of the world and its history. For Fray Juan, God was one who speaks in time, in life, in the world.

What I have tried to do in this book is to present this man, Fray Juan de la Cruz (1542–1591), as I have come to know him. I have written it for anyone who is interested in coming to know him as a human being who became, through and in his life, a man of God, a saint. I have written it to help those who would like to read his writings and understand them more clearly as guides on their journey to divine union and full human life.

My sources for this work have been the earliest manuscripts that relate what witnesses had to say about Fray Juan, as well as the first biographies and his own works. I have paid special attention to those witnesses who either had known Fray Juan personally or had lived with him. I have constructed the dialogues found herein from material found in these manuscripts. Those that are direct quotations are noted. In the closing sections of *John of the Cross: Man and Mystic,* I offer the reader of this new edition some advice on how to read the texts of Fray Juan de la Cruz as well as a section containing a brief introduction to each of his works and a selection of those texts. Finally, I have included an updated bibliography that concentrates on the main biographies of Fray Juan de la Cruz, a list of current English translations of his writings, and some works in English that will further help to deepen the reader's appreciation of Fray Juan and his teaching. My hope is that this new biography will help readers to find new and deeper meaning in the works of Fray Juan as they discover a new interpretation of his life. Moreover, readers may now fathom more personally the deep mystical union that Fray Juan proposes as God's gift to those who search authentically for Love.

Many people have been involved in helping me to bring this particular version to life. Of course, the first person I must thank is Sr. Madonna Ratliff, FSP, for her seeking me out and planting the thought of this publication in my mind. Moreover, Sr. Linda Salvatore, FSP, my editor, did a painstaking review of the book and offered her suggestions for improvement, for which I am extremely grateful. However, there are others, too, who played a most important role in the development of this book. I think of the late Dr. Kenneth Russell of Ottawa, Canada, who helped me so much in the original publication. Moreover, there are the Carmelite nuns in the many monasteries in the Philippines and the United States who invited me to share my thoughts on Fray Juan with them. In the process, they provided me with affirmation and new insights. The many students who participated in my courses and workshops on Fray Juan de la Cruz played their part in a deepening understanding of Fray Juan. I would also like to thank Ms. Marilyn Palermo, T.O.Carm., whose interest in my work and encouragement contributed to this book.

CHAPTER I

Juan de Yepes: The Young Man
(1542–1564)

THE DRAMA NEARED ITS COMPLETION. As the wintry winds blew through the narrow, cobblestone streets and pathways of Ubeda in southern Spain, the friars in a Carmelite monastery gathered in silence. In a cramped room on the upper level of the building lay an emaciated, tiny friar: Fray Juan de la Cruz. The labored breathing of the frail friar told those around him that the end was near. While faint whispers of prayer faded into silence, the candles held in the hands of his fellow friars cast eerie, moving shadows on the wall.

Suddenly the silence was shattered by the sound of the monastery bell calling the friars to the recitation of morning prayer. As he heard the familiar sound, Fray Juan opened his eyes and asked, "What was that bell for?" When one of the friars told him that it was the bell calling the brothers to the chapel for matins, he relaxed on the pillow and smiled peacefully. They might be praying here, but he knew he would be praying matins in eternity. Shortly after midnight, on December 13–14, 1591, death came as another step in the life of Fray Juan de la Cruz. He died as he had lived, surrounded by those who liked him and those who did not. In the forty-nine years of his life, he had puzzled people. He had angered some. He had entertained others. He had enemies and he had those who were devoted to him. He loved them all. Each formed part of that search he had embarked upon so early in his youth.

Family and Youth

The sixteenth century was one of the most dynamic in the history of Spain. This land of rustic beauty had achieved a greatness that would never again be equaled in her history. The famous ruling couple, Isabella and Ferdinand, struggled for and attained their goal of a united nation. Granada, taken from Moorish control in 1492, had yet to undergo the throes of the Inquisition, which struck fear in the hearts of so many Jews and followers of Islam. Nonetheless, it was now once more part of the Spanish nation.

The ports south of Granada on the Mediterranean bustled with activity. Dockworkers loaded provisions for the New World colonies, while others unloaded galleons bulging with treasured cargo from those distant lands. Like a colony of ants, the workers streamed in endless lines as they hustled crates and boxes on and off vessels. Those who had made the journey to the New World and lived to tell the tale entertained the crowds in the squares and taverns with stories of fantastic riches and high adventure.

At home, Spain developed. Indeed, she flourished. Her art, music, and life became the envy of all. Her king was Emperor of the Holy Roman Empire. Her influence extended to practically all of Europe and into the New World. Wealth abounded, at least for the nobles, but poverty oppressed the vast majority of the people. These two classes, the rich and the poor, existed side by side, separated, however, by the invisible barriers of their respective worlds. As a rule, people did not even attempt to bridge the chasm that kept them apart. Some, however, did dare to set conventions aside.

Gonzalo de Yepes and a woman called Catalina Alvarez were two such people. Gonzalo de Yepes came from an influential family in the region of Toledo in central Spain. For years family members had been clerics or *mercaderes*. Most were financiers whose large holdings enabled them to invest in manufacturing crafts and transportation. This automatically placed them among the upper class. Yet the family tree held secrets best hidden in that sensitive time. The Yepes family was *conversos*, that is, they were originally Jewish converts to Christianity.[1] To have had Jewish blood, even several generations earlier, made one suspect and hindered members of such a family from holding civil or ecclesiastical positions of power. The Inquisition kept such people under constant surveillance. Jealous citizens would often report them to the inquisitorial authorities, who would strip them of their property, honor, and position in the community. The Yepes hid their roots well.

Though the family itself was very wealthy, Gonzalo was not. An orphan, Gonzalo had gone to live with an uncle and his family. Eventually he worked for his uncle, which meant traveling a great deal, particularly in central and northern Spain.

It was in Fontiveros, a small town just north of Madrid, that Gonzalo, on a business trip to Medina del Campo on behalf of his uncle, met a young woman named Catalina Alvarez. Like Gonzalo, Catalina was originally from Toledo. A few years before Gonzalo entered her life, a widow from Fontiveros befriended Catalina and offered to share her home with the young woman. Since her parents had both died, Catalina believed she could start her life anew in this tiny village.

Gonzalo and Catalina fell in love. He could hardly wait to share his joy with his family, but they were horrified when he announced his plans to marry. They threatened to disown him and to number him among the dead if he went through with the proposed marriage. They knew Catalina was poor, but this was not the reason for their opposition.

In their eyes a far more serious reason demanded that they do all they could to stop the marriage. Catalina's background, too, had its secrets. She was rumored either to be the daughter of a Moorish slave or of someone who had been burned at the stake for Judaizing.[2] Gonzalo's marriage to her might provoke an investigation that could uncover their own Jewish background. The family regarded running such a risk unthinkable. The more obdurate they became, however, the more Gonzalo and Catalina were determined to go ahead.

These two young stalwarts were unique indeed. Though gentle and loving, Gonzalo was principled and determined. His love for Catalina was no infatuation that would fade as quickly as it had risen. For a man to give up a secure and comfortable life for an unknown future by marrying outside his class, love meant fidelity and sacrifice. Catalina was of the same mind.

Like her future husband, Catalina had been alone for a good part of her life. For her, marrying Gonzalo did not mean a guarantee of comfort and social status. Love was the principal element in their relationship—an interesting fact in an age when most marriages were arranged and love was not a necessary ingredient. Convinced that their love for each other would sustain them, they married around the year 1529.

Though their life together would be filled with moments of marvelous happiness, initially it was difficult. Disowned by his family, Gonzalo had to find new ways of making a living. Catalina taught him how to weave bonnets and thin veils for the ladies of the region. While weaving was not a trade that made one wealthy, it did provide for the basic necessities. The couple worked together long and hard as they started their family.

By 1542, Gonzalo and Catalina had three sons. Francisco, the eldest, born around 1530, was to play an extremely important role in the life of his youngest brother, Juan (later Fray Juan de la Cruz), who was born in 1542.[3] Their other son, Luis, was born sometime between Francisco and Juan.

The family survived, but barely managed to maintain itself at a subsistence level. Food was often scarce. What little they had to live on depended greatly upon their weaving skills, hard work, and the demand for their products. Their home became their factory. Colored threads, spools, and remnants were scattered about the largest of the rooms, which they also used as a living and dining room. Colors and odors blended, as did the sounds of the looms and shuttles moving along the unfolding cloth under Catalina and Gonzalo's agile fingers. As he got older, Juan would help dress the looms. Even though he was the youngest, he had to bear his share of the work and responsibilities.

Eventually, the strain of trying to earn enough for the family to live on, the sadness he felt at being cut off from his relatives, and the lack of substantial food took their toll on Gonzalo. After fifteen or so years of this draining life, he fell ill. His illness dragged on for several years, and his gradual decline caused the rest of the family to feel even more pressed to do their part to keep the family going.

Juan was deeply marked by his experience of being with and, in a way, caring for his ailing father during his last two years of life. In later years, first as an adolescent and then as a Carmelite friar, Juan would demonstrate that this experience had taught him how to be gentle and considerate in the care of the sick. But this closeness to a dying father was not the only childhood experience that influenced him.

His father's inability to play a role in the family's "cottage industry" made it imperative that Juan learn more about weaving. His mother taught him a few things so that he could help when she was busy caring for her dying husband. Juan remembered his weaving days when years later in one of his mystical poems he spoke of "...the veil of this sweet encounter."[4] The Spanish word translated as "veil" actually refers to the threads set into a weaver's loom. The natural events of work, life, and death made their imprint on the sensitive Juan de Yepes just as they do on every human being.

After two painful years of suffering, Gonzalo died. Catalina, left with three sons to care for, was desperate. What little money the family had saved had been quickly used up during Gonzalo's illness. The remaining four members of the Yepes family suffered the consequences: destitution. Catalina gathered her courage and set off with her sons to seek help from her husband's two brothers.

For Catalina, her children's well-being was first in her mind. Her hope, despite what she knew might be the outcome, was to have her brothers-in-law agree to take care of at least one or perhaps two of her sons. She thought and questioned herself about this as she and her sons made their way slowly southward to Toledo. Their first stop after the wearying journey on foot was in the neighborhood of Torrijos, not far from Toledo, where one of Juan's uncles was Archdeacon. The uncle listened to his sister-in-law's plea, but refused. He said he could not take the boys because they were too young, but Catalina knew there was more to it than that. She felt crushed. The division in the Yepes family caused by her marriage to Gonzalo so many years before had not been mended. The passing of the years and the death of Gonzalo had done nothing to calm the waters, at least in this particular person. As Catalina and her little troop made their way to Galvez (about fifteen miles from Toledo) to make another appeal, she wondered if the reception would be the same.

But things were very different in Galvez. Gonzalo's brother, also called Juan de Yepes, was a doctor. He showed a real interest in Catalina and her family. Since he and his wife had no children of their own, the idea of having a son appealed to him. So he offered to take care of the oldest of her children, Francisco, who by now was a teenager. This relieved Catalina greatly, for she saw that her eldest son now had a chance for a better life than she could ever offer him. After staying a few days in Galvez, Catalina left Francisco in her brother-in-law's care and returned to Fontiveros with Luis and Juan. Unfortunately, things did not turn out as ideally as she had hoped.

Back at home, Catalina continued her work, but wondered how Francisco was doing in his new home. After several months had passed without any news from him, she decided to go back to Galvez to see for herself. What she discovered shocked her. While the doctor had been extremely kind to Francisco, his wife made the boy work hard, kept him from going to school, and showed him no love whatever. Upon discovering Francisco's predicament, Catalina took him back with her despite the doctor's vow that things would be different.

Back in Fontiveros, things went from bad to worse. Catalina's weaving brought in little money. Moreover, Francisco, whose adolescence was well underway, seemed to be getting out of hand. He stayed out late and sometimes did not even come home at all. Catalina worried about him a great deal.[5] Then tragedy struck the family again. Luis died, probably from malnutrition.

Another move seemed to be the only way to survive, yet Catalina was reluctant to leave. Fontiveros held so many memories for her: she had met her husband there; her children had been born there; it was her home. But it was clear that she had to leave. So, she took her family to Arevalo (not very far from Fontiveros), where she and Francisco continued to work as weavers. Things were better, but still not good enough. Soon after their move to Arevalo (around 1550–1551), the family went to Medina del Campo.

Medina del Campo was a bustling city situated just northwest of Madrid on the main road leading from Salamanca to Valladolid. Trade fairs were held there twice a year, during May and October, with people from far-flung countries coming to participate in this biannual event. The merchants and financiers bartered goods from the East, spices and silks, books from distant countries, cloth, and exotic items from the New World. They also brought tales and news from far-off lands with them. Excitement filled the city during this time of festival as traders told of happenings in their countries of origin. Once one fair was over, preparations began immediately for the next. Juan grew up in this atmosphere of excitement and activity. At a time when news spread mainly through domestic and foreign visitors, Juan was in closer contact with what was occurring in different parts of the world than most Spaniards.

The importance of this period in Juan's life should not be underestimated. By the time his family had arrived in Medina del Campo, Juan was an impressionable nine-year-old. What he heard about the New World and what he saw in these annual trade fairs formed the young boy. He learned to listen and was continually discovering new and tantalizing things about the world far beyond the city's walls. In Medina del Campo, he could visit the Americas through the stories of those who had been there. He could smell the spices of the East with the merchants who brought them to sell. Through observation he knew what was happening politically, religiously, and socially in the municipal world around him. Submerged in the throbbing life of the city that became a major influence upon him, Juan became receptive to the new things he encountered and open to the deep values he would hold all his life. The city was his school. Yet his education was not limited to listening to those who bartered and traded goods in a medieval fair.

At this time in Medina del Campo there existed a school called the *Colegio de la Doctrina*. There, with other orphaned or poor children, Juan learned to read and write. Here he had his first real taste of formal learning and it was more or less a success. According to his brother, Juan learned to read and write just a few days after Catalina placed him in the school.[6] However, his teachers thought much less of his abilities in professional matters. They tried to teach him a trade—carpentry, tailoring, woodcarving, and painting—but he seemed unable to do well in any of these despite his eagerness to learn something that would enable him to help his family. These failures were disheartening for this conscientious boy of eleven or twelve.

His life continued in the same vein as that of any boy of his age and social class. He learned to serve for the Eucharist at the Convento de la Magdalena, which was the home of the Augustinian nuns. He worked and played, but, because of what had already happened in his life, he impressed others as being more sensitive and thoughtful than other boys his age. As he walked the cobblestone streets from his house to the convento, he thought about his future, his mother, and his work.

Las Bubas

Though Juan was just another small boy among many others in Medina del Campo, Don Alonso Alvarez de Toledo, the administrator of the Hospital de Nuestra Señora de la Concepción, more commonly called Las Bubas, took a special interest in him. The young fellow's maturity struck Don Alonso, and he decided to do something to help Juan.

Don Alvarez offered Juan a job as a nurse in his hospital. He had been observing young Juan at the convento for several weeks and realized that Juan's attitude and qualities were just what the hospital needed. When he asked the little boy if he would accept work at the hospital, Juan, who had painful memories of failing to learn a trade at the Colegio de la Doctrina, jumped at the chance, which would be of some help to his mother. In accepting the offer, Juan resolved that this would not be another failure.

When Juan began to work at Las Bubas, there were forty-five to fifty beds, sometimes more when patients brought in their own. All the beds, made of solid, wooden frames with straw mattresses and pillows stuffed with wool, were in one great room with no partitions between them.[7] Doña Teresa Enrriquez, Duchess of Maqueda, had founded the Hospital de Las Bubas in 1480 to treat people afflicted with ulcers and contagious diseases (this meant, in fact, those suffering from venereal diseases). It was one of the very few specialized hospitals in Medina del Campo. Because it cared for the poor with contractible illnesses, the hospital was located at some distance from the center of the city. Moreover, the biannual fairs attracted prostitutes and tempted the poor to make a little easy money by offering carnal services. This meant that the hospital was filled all year long. The physical, psychological, and social suffering of the patients impressed young Juan de Yepes in the adolescent, formative years when he lived and worked at Las Bubas.

Juan immersed himself in his work at once. His first concern was the sick. Though some of them were in terrible condition, he did all he could for them. Their open wounds and the anger and rejection they often expressed did not keep him from fulfilling his function. He would hold the weaker ones up to feed or bathe them and change their bandages when necessary. Many others would certainly have been repelled at the idea of touching them, but Juan was determined not to flinch. He wanted the sick to see that he was there to help them, and he showed this by drawing close to them. The dying found him at their side, encouraging and comforting them as much as possible. Juan would spend extra time with those who had no friends or relatives to visit them. When sadness and loneliness overcame them, Juan tried to make them happy.

In fact, Juan entertained them by telling stories and singing songs.[8] He loved to make people laugh, to lift up their spirits with music. He met their needs with as much care as he could muster at any given time—even if some days he could do little because he, too, was human and needed encouragement. Juan did not consider his hospital work as simply a job, but as a chance to help others, standing by them in their need. Everyone was amazed at the real compassion and gentleness of this teenager. With typical adolescent generosity, Juan responded to the attraction he felt toward those in need and tried to repress the revulsion that welled up in him as he washed the hideous sores and saw the human anguish in the patients' faces.

A person of great tenderness and sensitivity, Juan shared what others suffered. He was one of those people whose hearts immediately go out to others and whose lives are dominated by their love of those in great pain. His closeness to the destitute taught Juan the real values of life: he found the key to maturity, to becoming a man. He did not see the patients as the objects of his apostolic zeal. Rather, he saw them first and foremost as people. He respected them because he discovered that their way of relating to him and to each other taught him about life. They sensitized him to the beauty and ugliness of life. Juan found and related to God, the suffering God and the celebrating God, precisely in relating to them.

Yet he could not help but recoil at some of their diseases, and sometimes he tired of the constant drudgery involved in caring for the sick and just wanted to be alone. The opportunities Juan found to study in the loft of a barn on the hospital complex were moments he treasured and sought out as pure relief from the constant pressure of his work. When Don Alvarez, who had taken quickly to him, offered to let him pursue his education at a newly founded Jesuit school, Juan was thrilled.

Besides learning more about grammar, rhetoric, and metaphysics, Juan also met a young Jesuit, hardly older than himself, who became his teacher. Fray Juan Bonifacio became a friend as well as a mentor to Juan. They discussed the young boy's fears and the difficulties of his demanding life as a student-orderly. Fray Juan Bonifacio gave his eager student a serious grounding in the Latin and Spanish classics that took Juan beyond an elementary level.

Juan began to reflect on his life during the four years of his studies (1559–1563), in part as a result of Bonifacio's friendship and intellectual stimulation. He was puzzled by his family's poverty, his father's death, his mother's strength, and the suffering and inner strength he witnessed in the people he nursed at the hospital. But amid his confusion, he realized that the events of his life had meaning, and he knew God was involved, although he was not sure how. Only at the end of his lifetime would he be able to see how everything fitted together to form a pattern.

If Juan reflected on his life and daydreamed about his future, it was not because he had a lot of idle time on his hands. His scholastic work and nursing kept him busy, but he had other duties as well. Since the hospital served the poor, the patients could contribute little if anything to its upkeep. Funds had to be found somewhere by the hospital staff. Since the foundation of Las Bubas almost a hundred years earlier, one or more of the hospital's personnel had gone into the city to beg, making a special effort to collect funds during the trade fairs.[9] When Juan began working at Las Bubas, begging was one of his jobs. People would put money or donations in kind—bread, grain, food, cloth, candle wax, and the like—into his basket. This was a new experience for him. Though his family had been very poor, they had never had to go out and beg for help. Juan found this part of his duties very difficult. Only the love this sensitive young man felt for the people who depended upon him gave him the courage to ask for donations. He was determined to make a success of his begging, and the experience helped him to come to know himself a little better.

Juan's own situation was not much better than that of the patients he comforted. His sleeping accommodations were perfectly miserable. His "room" was simply a corner with a few twigs and branches spread across the floor. Yet he kept himself neat and clean. His concern for cleanliness, typical of Juan throughout his life, was quite unusual in an age when people bathed only a few times a year. The only quiet place where he could have some privacy to study and to think about his life was a bug-infested loft. One day his mother found him there, so absorbed in his reading that he was oblivious to the insects crawling around him. The time he spent at the hospital at Medina del Campo taught Juan the meaning of asceticism—to be free from all things in order to love them all the more deeply and truly, even passionately.

Although Juan was to remain small in stature—about four feet, ten inches—his spirit grew and his personality developed in the few years he worked at the hospital. His love for others and his concern with alleviating their suffering became more and more important. God was a "natural" part of everyday life in sixteenth-century Spain, but God was more than this to young Juan de Yepes. As he struggled with the troublesome aspects of growing up, Juan had lost sight of God, but he then rediscovered his Creator and learned to communicate with God more deeply, as God did with him, in all the daily events of his life. God was becoming his intimate friend. Indeed, he had fallen in love with God.

When he was twenty-one years old, Juan began to think of making another kind of life for himself. It was about this time that Don Alvarez approached Juan with another offer. Alvarez wanted Juan to be ordained as a chaplain to the hospital. His role would be to celebrate the Eucharist and serve the patients in a sacramental way. This would open new possibilities for Juan and his family. If he accepted the offer, he would finally be able to give his mother more substantial financial help. He certainly would not be rich, but he would have the means to give her a chance to rest a little. It would also mean he could continue to help the sick not only physically—as he had done until now—but also spiritually. The fact that he already knew the hospital and its doctors and nurses would make things easier. It would be fascinating, he thought, and he already liked the work. The more he thought about it, the clearer it became that this could very well be the ideal place for him. Yet, something within him resisted the offer. Finally, after much thought and prayer, Juan decided that the chaplaincy at Las Bubas was not for him.

A Carmelite Vocation

Around 1560 the Carmelites had founded a monastery called the Convento de Santa Ana in Medina del Campo. In 1563, when Juan finished his program of studies with the Jesuits, he made up his mind to join the Carmelites. For one reason or another, he did not tell Don Alvarez of his decision, but secretly left the hospital and went to the monastery. On that warm day, as he walked toward the Carmelite monastery, he thought about his past life and his future. All that he had been given—the events, the people—filled his mind. He was too gentle and sensitive not to remember those gifts of the past as he began a new direction in his life. But was it really new?

When he arrived at the small monastery, Juan asked to be received in their community. He was immediately admitted, and the superior clothed him with the habit and gave him the tonsure to mark his new clerical state. Thus, he began his year of novitiate right away. While little is known of this yearlong training within the tradition of the Order of Carmel, we do know that the monastery at this time was only a small house. Juan's room was tiny, narrow, and dark. During this year of novitiate, Juan practiced the Rule of the community very strictly: abstinence, fasting, all-night vigils, discipline, and prayer. His determination and devotion made him diligent in the practice of his religious life, and he seemed to impress those who knew him with his simplicity and the consistent care he took even in the least important of tasks.

Whenever he could, Juan sought out solitude. While he needed the pleasure of being with other people, he also needed to be alone and quiet. Both facets of life constituted important dimensions of growth for his personality and spiritual life. Juan's deep love for silence and solitude caused his brothers in community to consider him somewhat strange. The severity of his observance set him apart from the others and he did not really become one of the group. While they admired him, the brothers also thought that he was too devout. Later, when he became a superior, his early reputation preceded him and many of the brothers feared his appointment because they thought he would be too severe. They discovered instead that his austere beginnings had produced a different kind of person than they had expected.

The year of novitiate ended much too quickly for Juan. Profession of vows took place sometime after May 21, 1564.[10] That same year, the Very Reverend Father Rubeo became Superior General of the Order. Juan, or Fray Juan de Santo Matía as he was now known in the Carmelites, celebrated his commitment to this community in the presence of Padre Alonso Ruiz, the superior of Santa Ana, and his friend Don Alonso Alvarez. A new phase in Juan's life began.

CHAPTER II

The Young Carmelite and the Reform
(1564–1572)

WHEN HE FINISHED HIS NOVITIATE, young Fray Juan de Santo Matía traveled to Salamanca where he prepared himself further for what was to be his new life among the Carmelites. Late in the year 1564, when the Carmelite friar arrived in the University city, Salamanca's cold winter winds were already blowing through its narrow streets. In the drab wintry season, this center of Spain's intellectual learning appeared rather unwelcoming. Yet, this did not dampen Juan's enthusiasm. He took full advantage of his appointment for study that his superiors had offered him.

Salamanca vibrated with new trends and unparalleled opportunities for learning. All Europe knew of the university's vitality. Though Latin was supposed to be the vehicle of conversation, the new pride that Spaniards took in their language was pushing it aside. Changes such as this were typical of the ferment in a dynamic era that excited the young students of literature and philosophy. Juan fell in love with the harmonious cadences of the Castilian language. Students often composed their own songs in this romance language. Could Fray Juan have done the same? Possibly, since he had entertained the sick in Medina del Campo with his songs. We also know that in later life he wrote a poem based on a Castilian ballad, and that he often sang songs as he traveled from one place to another.[1] Here in Salamanca his interest in music kept pace with his love of literature and the Spanish language. He was clearly a student deeply influenced by the atmosphere prevalent at the university at the time, where only 750 of the university's 7,000 students studied theology.

Noise and color filled the streets snaking through the old city as the lay students joked, talked, and teased each other on their way to class—the only time for any levity since the discipline in their residences and the university itself was terribly rigid. All the students contributed to the rich riot of color. The major schools had special colors, which the students wore. Before and after classes the streets of Salamanca were filled with people wearing cloaks of gray, blue, and purple mingling with the white capes of the Carmelites and the colorful habits of the different religious communities that had houses of study in the city. The same striking mélange of colors appeared after classes when professors stood by a pillar and answered students' questions. Fray Juan was certainly part of this inquisitive crowd, for he constantly sought to understand more of the world that was unfolding before him daily.

He attended classes at the university, where the more gifted of the Carmelite friars went, though he was also studying at the Carmelite Colegio of San Andrés situated on the banks of the Tormes River outside the city walls. In the scholastic year 1564–1565, the register of the university noted the presence of "Fray Juan de Santo Matía natural de Medina del Campo del obispado de Salamanca" ("Fray Juan de Santo Matía, native of Medina del Campo the Diocese of Salamanca"), and he continued to be registered there as an arts student until 1567. In 1567–1568, the register listed Juan as a priest and theologian.[2] He was so successful in his studies that his superior named him prefect of students with the responsibility of teaching and helping the other brothers in their studies. All these experiences helped shape Fray Juan's personality.

In the Colegio de San Andrés, Fray Juan's living quarters were Spartan. His room was small, dark, and narrow. It had a little window that opened onto the chapel, and a small opening in the roof to let in some light. A few boards, without a mattress or pillow, served as his bed. Juan conscientiously followed the stricter ancient Carmelite Rule by his own choice. Some of the other friars who neither followed a personal program of asceticism nor showed much zeal for the common Rule avoided Fray Juan because they thought him too serious. Just as in Medina del Campo, his severe asceticism isolated him from his brothers. His youth and zeal led him into a situation where the friars considered him overly strict and perhaps even fanatical. Strangely enough, his studies at Salamanca gradually broke Juan out of the "angelism" to which he was prone during this youthful period. Fray Juan could have rejected the beauty of the literature he studied and the various other trends of the time as earthly things he should put aside. But his temperament was too strongly drawn in this direction. He instinctively knew these realities could not be evil, though he was not yet comfortable with the pleasure he took in them. Only later in life would he realize deep in his own personality that he had to integrate the wholeness of the world into the process of learning to love God, but this realization was taking root even now.

At twenty-two, Fray Juan saw that he could not escape his aloofness no matter how he tried to be kind toward others. He was determined, silent, and studious. In fact, we could say he did not seem to be a very pleasant person to have around. If he came along when some of the brothers were speaking at a time they should have been silent, they would run away immediately. They knew if they stayed that he would give them a little sermon about the Rule. In fact, the other friars avoided him whenever possible. Thus, Fray Juan was alone a good deal of the time. Was this really the Juan of the Hospital de Las Bubas? Yes, but a real lack of balance in his attitudes and activities had developed. He still perceived spiritual life as "spiritual" or otherworldly, and consequently he developed a severe, harsh attitude toward earthly life. His determination to follow the Rule strictly did not endear him to his fellow students. He was one of the fervent types to be found in any novitiate or scholasticate—filled with a desire to be holy, but with an inhuman notion of holiness.

However, this was simply too contrary to Juan's sensitive nature to last very long. He felt too strongly drawn by the fascination and beauty of the real world around him to deny its goodness. It gnawed at him. In an effort to end his yearning for it, he increased his ascetical practices as if they could free him of all this earthliness. He may have felt it was necessary to get out of the world through disciplining his body, fasting, vigils, and long prayers, but unconsciously he was discovering how incarnate he was and how necessary this was to his becoming one with the God of Jesus. His Salamancan period was not wasted; his coming to God utilized all the learning experiences of his life.

By 1567, Fray Juan de Santo Matía was sufficiently advanced in his studies to be ordained. In August of that year, he returned to Medina del Campo for the celebration of his first Eucharist among his relatives and the friends of his earlier days. The trip from Salamanca to Medina del Campo, though not long, provided him with time for some serious thinking. Fray Juan had long been reflecting on the possibility of adopting another lifestyle. The life at Carmel did not seem strict enough for him. He was not passing judgment on others. He simply wanted to make more than the little effort the Rule of Carmel demanded of him.

While in Salamanca, he had nurtured a secret desire. No doubt his isolation from the other friars, which his own practices led to, played its role here too. Since he was unable to communicate freely with his fellow Carmelites in San Andrés, solitude was more or less imposed on him. It was natural that he should begin to feel alienated from a group with whom he could not share his hopes and ideals. This sense of not belonging had been growing in him since his novitiate days. The little friar had not really made friends in his Carmelite community, and, for such a sensitive man, this was a heavy cross. To be unable to share his intimate thoughts or desires with a like-minded friend must have been extremely painful. Not the open and loving person he would later become, few, if any, felt attracted to this little "saint." His strictness excluded him from the fellowship that normally develops in a community setting. His superior intellectual abilities and his appointment as prefect effectively separated him from the group. It is no wonder then that by the time of the celebration of his first Eucharist, Fray Juan was seriously contemplating joining the Carthusians.

Juan's hopes settled on the Carthusian Monasterio del Paular, which was situated near Segovia. Here he felt he could live out a saintly life as he then envisioned it: he could spend his life withdrawn from "worldly commerce," quiet and alone with God. The Carthusian Rule did not accentuate community life, so he felt he would be quite happy. No longer would he have to be different. Most of all, he could devote himself entirely to God. But could the young man who had given himself completely to the sick in Las Bubas and to the students at San Andrés really isolate himself even for God? Perhaps at that time Fray Juan saw that God did not just dwell in the infinite beyond. Rather God came and comes in time and in people. This realization was surely in the back of Juan's mind as he thought about his future. Although going to Paular seemed the right thing to do, he still felt unsettled. Fray Pedro de Orozco, whom Juan had taken with him to Medina del Campo, knew that Fray Juan had to meet la Madre Teresa de Avila. Therefore, he arranged a meeting, which would become a key event in the history of the Order of Carmel and of Christian mysticism.

On August 14, 1567, *la Madre,* as she was called, went to Medina del Campo to establish her second monastery of sisters. There were some difficulties in getting a house, which they gradually overcame. From her we learn what transpired during her meeting with Fray Antonio, the prior who helped her get a house.

> Now, with this I began to calm down because we were able to keep strict enclosure, and we began to recite the Hours. The good prior [Fray Antonio de Heredia] hurried very much with the repair of the house, and he suffered many trials. Nonetheless, the work took two months. But the house was repaired

in such a way that we were able to live there in a reasonably good manner for several years.... While in
Medina, I was still concerned about the monasteries
for friars, and since I didn't have any, as I said, I didn't
know what to do. So I decided to speak about the
matter very confidentially with the prior there to see
what he would counsel me, and this I did. He was
happy to know of it and promised me he would be
the first. I took it that he was joking with me and
told him so. For although he was always a good friar,
recollected, very studious, and fond of his cell—in
fact, he was a learned man—it didn't seem to me he
was the one for a beginning like this. Neither would
he have the courage or promote the austerity that
was necessary, since he was fragile and not given to
austerity. He assured me very much and asserted that
for many days the Lord had been calling him to a
stricter life. Thus, he had already decided to go to the
Carthusians, and they had already told me that they
would accept him. Despite all this, I was not completely satisfied. Although I was happy to hear what
he said, I asked that we put it off for a while and that
he prepare by putting into practice the things he
would be promising....[3]

Not long after, sometime in September or October,
Madre Teresa de Jesús had heard of Fray Juan de Santo Matía
from his companion, Fray Pedro de Orozco. Fray Pedro
arranged a meeting within that two-month period.

Madre Teresa was already fifty-two years old and had
long been involved in the establishment of the Reform of the
female branch of the Carmelite Order. Her ideal was to establish some monasteries where the nuns would follow the prim-

itive Rule rather than the mitigated one, which all had followed before her movement started. She had recently received permission from the Superior General of the Order, Padre Juan Bautista Rubeo (Rossi), to start two convents of the Reform, in addition to the Convento de San José, which she had founded several years earlier in Avila. Medina del Campo was the first of these new convents. The excerpt quoted from her *Foundations* shows that she was anxious to start the Reform of the male branch of the Order.

The primitive Rule of the Carmelites was rather strict, but it had been made easier through the centuries as zeal diminished and the accent shifted from a more contemplative to an apostolic orientation. Pope Eugenius IV mitigated the Rule in 1432, and other popes eased it even more. Teresa decided to return to the primitive Rule which, among other things, made contemplative prayer and silence the most important features of the lifestyle. Teresa's Reform movement reinstated total abstinence from meat and lengthy fasting from September 14 (the feast of the Exaltation of the Holy Cross) to Easter. Part of the Reform also involved a change in the religious dress. Rather than the graceful, soft, and full habits of the Carmelites of the mitigated Rule, the nuns and later the friars of Teresa's Reform would wear a shorter, less ample habit made of a coarse, heavy material. Furthermore, they would no longer wear shoes as the mitigated Rule allowed. Thus, the Reform friars and nuns came to be known as *Discalced* Friars and Nuns, while the others were popularly known as the *Calced*. While the nuns of the Reform would remain cloistered, the friars would continue to be committed to an apostolic activity consisting of preaching, celebrating the liturgy, and spiritual direction, though it was Teresa's intention that they maintain a deeply contemplative lifestyle. This was her hope for the future as she met with Fray Juan de Santo Matía.

This young friar, only twenty-five years old at the time, bent upon becoming part of a community that would be more austere, and thus more to his liking, was bound to be fascinated by the goals of Madre Teresa. Madre Teresa has left us a description of their quiet meeting:

> A little later it happened that a young Father came there who was studying in Salamanca. He came along with another, as his companion [Fray Pedro de Orozco], who told me great things about the life this Father was leading. The young Father's name was Fray John of the Cross. I praised our Lord. And when I spoke with this young friar, he pleased me very much. I learned from him how he also wanted to go to the Carthusians. Telling him what I was attempting to do, I begged him to wait until the Lord would give us a monastery and pointed out the great good that would be accomplished if in his desire to improve he were to remain in his own Order and that much greater service would be rendered to the Lord. He promised me he would remain as long as he wouldn't have to wait long. When I saw that I already had two friars to begin with, it seemed to me the matter was taken care of; although I still wasn't so satisfied with the prior, and thus I waited a while, and waited also for the sake of finding a place where they could begin.[4]

She was excited at the prospect of having this young, determined friar as part of the Reform. Fray Juan continued to impress her over the years, though not always in a comfortable way. He was as strong and determined as she was. Though she did not realize it immediately, it was not long before she came to see that she had finally met her match in a man. All the other men she had met were simply overwhelmed by her presence and abilities, and they acceded to her wishes with respect and admiration. Fray Juan de Santo Matía, on the other hand, would clearly inform her of his opinion whether or not it agreed with hers.[5] As early as 1568, she herself said that he irritated her and that they sometimes had arguments when their opinions differed.[6] It is not surprising, therefore, that though she knew Juan would be a most faithful and helpful servant of the Reform, she chose another protégé to be the superior: Fray Jeronimo de la Madre de Dios (Gracian). This young, energetic, and handsome man, who had a very real zeal for the community, was especially perfect in la Madre's eyes because he always agreed with her. Fray Juan was the only one she could never really control. No doubt Teresa appreciated him for this reason, but at the same time she did not want him in a position where his ideas could cause her difficulties. Nonetheless, as a result of their meeting Fray Juan was to become an essential part of the Reform. Initially, however, he said nothing about this new turn in his life.

Fray Juan returned to Salamanca in November of 1567 to study theology. Madre Teresa, meanwhile, busied herself establishing other houses and getting ready for the new one, which would house the men of the Reform. By May of 1568, a Señor Rafael Mejia gave her a "house" at Duruelo, not far from Avila. Toward the end of June, Teresa went with a companion to see it. Her description of that twenty-five-mile journey and what she saw is remarkable.

Although we left in the morning, we got lost because we didn't know the road; and since the place is little known, we couldn't get much information about where it was. Thus, our traveling that day was very trying and the sun was very hot. When we thought we were near, we discovered we had just as far to go. I always remember the tiredness we felt and the wrong roads we took on that journey. The result was that we arrived shortly before nightfall. When we entered the house it was in such a state that we dared not remain there that night; it wasn't at all clean and was filled with vermin. It had a fairly good entrance way, a room double in size, a loft, and a small kitchen. This was all we had for our monastery. I figured that the entrance way could serve as a chapel, the loft as the choir, which would adapt well, and the room for sleeping. My companion, although much better than I and very fond of penance, couldn't bear the thought of my planning to found a monastery there and said to me: "Surely, Mother, there isn't a soul, however good, that could put up with this. Don't even consider it." The Father, who came with me, although he agreed with my companion, did not oppose me since I had told him my intentions. We went to spend the night in the church, although not in vigil because we were exhausted.[7]

This rather depressing hovel was to be the new home and the beginning of the Reform for Fray Juan de Santo Matía. But first he needed to talk with Teresa about the new spirit of the community he was about to start.

For Fray Juan the year 1567 to 1568 felt like a long period of waiting. He had just had time for a brief meeting with la

Madre in late October 1567 before she was obliged to leave Medina del Campo to regulate the affairs of the Reform. Teresa's departure left Juan and Fray Antonio with a few days of leisure before returning to Salamanca. They used the time to discuss their hopes for the success of the Reform and to plan the life they were to share. They differed in age and personality. Fray Juan was more retiring and quiet, while Fray Antonio was outgoing and talkative. As they spoke, they found more and more that the ideal of living the primitive Rule delighted them both. When they considered all the circumstances, they discovered they both needed the support their newly found companionship provided. Their conversations, and those they had had with Madre Teresa, became the continual subject of Fray Juan's thoughts. For the time being, their plans remained secret.

Being a conscientious and determined person, Fray Juan immersed himself in his studies of theology. The professors who taught at Salamanca had the perfect student in this small friar. He was not one to simply accept what a professor told him. He would reflect upon the ideas presented, search out the texts, and study them carefully. Over the years, he had developed his studies in such a serious and exacting way that they had become a form of prayer.

Juan spent his last year in Salamanca waiting restlessly. The cloisters and their ornate facades had lost their appeal. Self-doubt clouded his anticipation. Would he be strong enough to live the Reform? Was this really God's will or his own? Was he simply trying to run away from other responsibilities? The questions would come, go, and come back again, and he always took them seriously. Yet, despite appearances, these doubts never destroyed Juan's underlying conviction that this was indeed the way in which he had to move. He sensed deep within himself that somehow this was right for him. He clung to this conviction when he returned to Medina del Campo in the summer of 1568, just after he turned twenty-six.

By July 1, 1568, Madre Teresa had arrived in Medina del Campo on her way from Malagon. She had already seen Duruelo and had informed both Fray Juan and Fray Antonio about its miserable condition, but this did not dampen their spirits. They wanted to get on with the new foundation and finally commit themselves to the new life that they had been waiting so long to begin. Nonetheless, before embarking on this adventure, they had a few minor details to settle. The delay, however, gave Fray Juan time to prepare more intensely for the coming years.

He and Madre Teresa had a month to talk over the Reform before the two of them left with some others for Valladolid. They discussed the basic spirit behind the Reform movement, and Fray Juan thus received some insight into the importance and fundamental thrust behind la Madre's actions and her hopes. These discussions intensified as they traveled the twenty-eight miles from Medina del Campo to Valladolid, where la Madre hoped to establish yet another convent of her sisters.

The small group of travelers included six nuns, a young girl who was about to join them, Fray Juan, Madre Teresa, and the former chaplain to San José, the first Discalced convent Madre Teresa established in Avila. Each of the travelers experienced a mini-novitiate as Madre Teresa interspersed periods of silence and prayer with discussions about their way of life as Discalced Carmelites. For Fray Juan, this novitiate continued during the following weeks as he and Teresa tried to obtain the necessary authorizations to establish the monastery at Duruelo. This period became his introduction to a whole new lifestyle that would be his for the next twenty-three years.

Duruelo

With the necessary documents in hand, and a few things with which to start his new life, Fray Juan left Valladolid for Avila in early September 1568. Not long afterward, Fray Juan and a lay brother, Fray José de Cristo, left Avila on the road to Duruelo.

Though he had not officially taken the vows of the Discalced, Fray Juan already looked like one, wearing the habit la Madre and her nuns had made for him and requested he wear. Though he was so short, he looked impressive in the coarse, dark gray-brown scapular and cassock, over which he wore the modified version of the flowing white cape so familiar to those who knew the Carmelites. The austere clothing fit perfectly with his dark skin, long narrow nose, and thin face topped with a receding hairline. The rosary hanging from his belt clicked quietly as he and Fray José walked barefoot toward their new home.

When they arrived in Duruelo, they discovered how accurate la Madre's description of the house had been. It was rather desolate, surrounded by dusty and gray fields already divested of their crops. The building they would call a monastery was no more than a tumbled-down barn. But when Madre Teresa's companion had said that no one could be expected to live in a place like that, she had not counted on Fray Juan's determination and strength. Yet even he was taken aback by the condition of the building. It was filthy and in a state of near collapse. Much needed to be done. Fray Juan, who was always so clean and neat, sensed a natural repulsion as he first entered these "ruins." Nonetheless, he would not be overcome by something as trivial as a dirty, run-down house. The two new friars set to work immediately, sweeping, washing, nailing up boards, and repairing the whole structure. But they were not about to simply rebuild. They would have to set up the rooms and add certain human touches like the decorations appropriate to their lifestyle. Someone who knew Fray Juan very well and had lived with him later in his life describes what the two friars did to the house in these words:

> It had only a porch and a double room with an attic and a small kitchen with its own entrance. They remodeled it in this way. They made the porch into the church. The lower room they made into a dormitory leaving space near the church part for two confessionals.... In the dormitory they put their beds which, for better or worse, were no more than straw and an old blanket placed on the floor while for pillows they used pieces of wood with two or three other pillows made of coarse material filled with straw. They divided the kitchen in two parts: in one they made a refectory with a table covered with place mats for each monk...in the other was the kitchen and utensils. The attic they made into a choir room.... But when the snow came, it fell into the attic itself.[8]

To turn this old barn into a monastery required hard work and a good deal of time. Fray Juan decided to make sure people knew what the barn had become by putting a large wooden cross in the field in front of it and another cross on the front door. They put more crosses in different places in the small, renovated barn, including a small paper one that Fray Juan himself hung above the holy water font. In imitation of their Master, they wanted their life to be one of self-sacrifice for God and the world. They did not aim so much at death to the world as to the abandonment of all that hindered them from loving in the world that God who had created and loved the world. For Fray Juan everything in creation found its place in a freeing process in which the human person would find God more fully.

The two brothers in Carmel worked and prayed as they awaited the formal opening of their monastery. This took place on November 28, 1568. The provincial, Fray Alonso Gonzalez, had arrived the day before with Fray Antonio, who was to join the new group of *Discalced* men. On seeing Fray Juan already dressed in the habit of the Reform, Fray Alonso felt disappointment over Fray Juan not having waited for him. However, his sadness and anger soon passed as they gathered to celebrate the Eucharist to officially mark the beginning of the new venture.

At the end of the Eucharist, presided over by the provincial, Fray Juan, Fray Antonio, and Fray José renounced the mitigated Rule they had followed and promised to live according to the primitive Rule. It was a new beginning and as a sign of that they took new names. From now on Fray Juan de San Matía would be known as Fray Juan de la Cruz, while Fray Antonio Heredia would be called Fray Antonio de Jesús. Fray José and two others also joined the community.

This group of five now began to live the new Rule. Fray Antonio became prior, and Fray Juan de la Cruz was named master of novices. Silence formed a major part of their lives, especially between compline (night prayer) and prime. This provided them with an atmosphere for the contemplation they hoped to practice and foster. In addition to the two hours of mental prayer, which they performed in common every day, they spent much of their time praying privately and meditating on the law of the Lord. They fasted regularly from the feast of the Exaltation of the Cross (September 14) until Easter, as the primitive Rule required.

Fray Juan de la Cruz was filled with a joyful peace during this time. Everything seemed perfect to him. He could not imagine a more deeply contemplative life. Fray Juan possessed the delights of a new beginning in Duruelo. Whether he was working in the fields, praying, or preaching in the surrounding villages, everything seemed to fit perfectly into a harmonious pattern. While he saw God in all of this, he also knew that this could not be equated with God. In time, Fray Juan would understand this even better.

The atmosphere that so affected visitors when they beheld these friars in their humble monastery can be felt in la Madre's account of her rather quick visit there in early 1569.

> The following Lent, while on my way to the foundation in Toledo, I passed by there. When I arrived in the morning, Father Fray Antonio was sweeping the doorway to the church with that joyful expression on his face that he always has. I said to him: "What's this, my Father; what has become of your honor?" Telling me of his great happiness, he answered with these words: "I curse the day I had any." When I entered the little church, I was astonished to see the spirit the Lord had put there. And it wasn't only I,

for the two merchants, my friends from Medina who had accompanied me there, did nothing else but weep. There were so many crosses, so many skulls! I never forget a little cross made for the holy water fount from sticks with a paper image of Christ attached to it; it inspired more devotion than if it had been something very expertly carved. The choir was in the loft. In the middle of the loft the ceiling was high enough to allow for the recitation of the Hours, but one had to stoop low in order to enter and to hear Mass. There were in the two corners facing the church two little hermitages, where one could do no more than either lie down or sit. Both were filled with hay because the place was very cold, and the roof almost touched one's head. Each had a little window facing the altar and a stone for a pillow; and there, too, the crosses and skulls.[9]

The simplicity and poverty in which they all lived gave the friars a joy nothing else could. They devoted themselves to prayer and the service of God and enjoyed it immensely. The cross, which was the sign of their liberation, could be seen everywhere, reminding them of how they would grow in this new lifestyle.

The presence of Fray Juan's family added to his joy. Nothing could stand in the way of the intimacy the Yepes family shared. If anything, the fact that the youngest member of the family had started this new form of life drew the family even closer together. Consequently, shortly after Duruelo had become the first monastery of the reformed life, Fray Juan de la Cruz' mother, brother, and sister-in-law came there to be with him. His mother cooked the meals at the little monastery while his sister-in-law washed the linens and clothes. Francisco cleaned and arranged the rooms of the monastery.[10] Living and working there provided them with the necessities of life at a time when they were in great need. In his love and concern for them, Fray Juan saw to their comfort. Moreover, it meant a great deal to simply have them with him. His deep, constant love for his mother and brother impressed everyone.[11]

Both Fray Antonio and Fray Juan de la Cruz would go out to the surrounding towns to preach the Word to the people. When Francisco was at the monastery, he would accompany his brother on this apostolate. If the journey were a fair distance, they would take a little bread with them and eat it seated by some stream or by the roadside on their way back. Sometimes the pastor of the parish invited them both to stay and eat with him. But Fray Juan always politely refused such offers and went on his way. When asked why he did not stay, Fray Juan would reply gently but with conviction: "It is not good that I be paid for my service to God and his people."[12]

Fray Juan's homilies reflected his own gentleness and encouraged the people to live what they believed. He wanted them to know that Jesus should be the center of their lives—neither persons nor things should take the place of Jesus in their hearts.[13]

Whatever his subject, Juan impressed the people who heard him. They often said that in some unique way they felt the very reality he was trying to communicate to them.[14] The people did not hear just words; they sensed a real participation in the reality of which Juan spoke. In order to do this, God must be alive in the homilist. Fray Juan de la Cruz had that gift. However, since he found the praises of the people quite embarrassing, he would attempt to leave secretly immediately after his homily so that he would avoid hearing the people's reaction. The return trip to the monastery, like the one going, was quiet, reflective, and prayerful. This did not mean, however, that Fray Juan de la Cruz trudged along the dirt roads of Spain with downcast eyes and a stern face. Even on these short forays outside the monastery, the world was an invitation to and an occasion for prayer. What Juan saw made him conscious that God was present not only deep within himself but also in the world of which he felt himself a part. Juan's God was a God of creation, joyfully present in time. In Duruelo, Fray Juan de la Cruz lived the Rule of Carmel; its incarnation in every conscious moment of his life made him the holy one of the Discalced.

Mancera and Pastrana

Fray Juan de la Cruz lived and worked in Duruelo for over a year, but he was not to stay in this idyllic setting for long. In June of 1570, the whole Duruelo community moved to Mancera de Abajo. Here, about three miles from Duruelo, a wealthy man had offered the Discalced a house just when the arrival of new candidates made the building at Duruelo much too small. Fray Juan continued to instruct the novices for a while after the transfer of the community to Mancera, but it was not long before the community would need his talents in yet another monastery of Discalced Friars.

Again, the generosity of some local people enabled the friars to open a monastery in Pastrana in 1569. The students in the university town of Alcala de Henares, not far from Madrid and only about thirty-five miles southeast of Pastrana, had heard about the life of contemplation that these friars were leading. Many of them were favorably impressed and wanted to join. By October 1570, the community asked Fray Juan to go to Pastrana for a short visit to establish a novitiate there.

The trip to Pastrana provides us with some important insights for a deeper understanding of Fray Juan de la Cruz. Accompanied by Fray Pedro de los Angeles, Fray Juan walked along the dusty roads chilled by the fall winds that were already starting to blow. Fray Juan gave Fray Pedro a few *platicas* or concise sayings concerning life, God, or the world. They actually sounded like summaries of what Fray Juan had come to know through his own life. Even more interesting is the fact that along the way they begged for money and food, but not for themselves. They would take the money they collected and then disburse it along the way to the poor whom they met. Furthermore, in keeping with their idea of simplicity they would always sleep in very poor houses or barns. If someone offered them a decent place to spend the night or to rest, Fray Juan gently refused. He possessed a very real sense of service as well as of poverty. He wanted to share the lot of the poor he saw about him and whom he had known all his life. Though this approach to realistic religious poverty appealed to him personally, he did not demand that his brothers follow his example. They were free to accept offers of food and comfortable accommodations on trips outside the monastery, but Fray Juan regarded poverty as a means to break down the social barriers that religious erected between themselves and Spain's oppressed and poor. Through his rather strict personal lifestyle, he always remained at ease with the poor and maintained his freedom to live fully in the world. His contemplative life was not lived outside the world; on the contrary, it was based on a real love for the world. Though many in his time simply prayed for the poor, Fray Juan did something for them.

Soon after their arrival in Pastrana, Fray Juan set to work. He used his experience in Duruelo and Mancera to set up the novitiate and prepared Fray Gabriel de la Asunción to act as novice master. When he completed his work, he and his companion returned to Mancera. They had stayed in Pastrana only about one month, but it was long enough to establish the structures needed to promote the ideal of the Discalced Carmelite Friars. He remained in Mancera until April of 1571.

Then the Discalced sent Juan to become the rector of the Colegio de San Cyrilo in Alcala de Henares. Here he organized the residence so that friars could live according to the primitive Rule of the Discalced. However, in the early spring of 1572 something came to his attention that forced him to return to Pastrana.

The novice master in Pastrana was now Fray Angel de San Gabriel. His strictness and the silly demands he imposed on the novices not only disturbed the monastery itself but also caused the people of the town to ridicule and dislike the friars. Fray Angel expected the novices to obey him without question, and to test their obedience he would command them to go about the town dressed in rags and acting as if they were madmen. This conduct brought the scorn of the townspeople upon them and the community. Fray Angel also ordered them to press the townsfolk to come to the monastery. It was not long before word spread; fewer and fewer candidates came to be admitted, while some novices actually left the community. The situation, if left unchecked, could do great harm to the new communities of Discalced Friars. The superiors asked Fray Juan de la Cruz to look into the matter and to correct whatever had gone wrong.

On his arrival, Fray Juan began to correct the extreme asceticism that Fray Angel had ordered the novices to practice, but he did this with a great deal of diplomatic tact. He spoke gently to the community on the real value of their lives as friars of the primitive Rule that accentuated prayer and the cloister. Then he set about changing things. He put a stop to all the penitential extravagances outside the monastery and moderated the penances and mortifications within it. Fray Juan was only interested in those practices that succeeded in freeing individuals for authentic love and service to God. In Fray Juan's opinion what had been going on before had nothing to do with God; the practices had become ends in themselves. With his concern for all, his gentleness, and his sound logic, Fray Juan de la Cruz reestablished a healthy situation for a solid introduction to the primitive Carmelite life. Now he was ready for the new assignment that would end abruptly and introduce him to an experience that would color his whole life.

CHAPTER III

Avila and the Monastery of the Encarnación
(1572–1577)

AVILA, THE HOME OF FRAY JUAN FROM 1572 to 1577, is still very much like it was in the sixteenth century. The fortified city is perched on a hilltop overlooking miles of plains that separate it from the Sierra de Grados Mountains in the distance. Its ancient walls and towers stand majestically against the searing summer sun. The red-tiled roofs of the churches and houses within the city add to the burnt-autumn appearance of this marvelous medieval city. These structures speak of strength, power, and determination. It is no surprise that it was the home of Madre Teresa de Jesús.

In 1571, thirty-five years had passed since she had joined the Carmelite Convent of the Encarnación. True, she had started the Reform in 1561, and had, therefore, lived outside that convent most of that decade. Yet the Encarnación, situated outside the city walls, had been her home for a good part of her life. The monastery was so poor that the sisters often had very little to eat. Sometimes conditions became so bad that the sisters had to temporarily stay with relatives or friends in the city. Years of this regime had eroded the religious discipline of the convent. Some of the sisters had been sent to the convent by their families, and consequently did not think much of their vocation. They were quite happy to have periods of freedom outside the monastic framework. Many expressed their displeasure at the Reform of Teresa de Jesús. After all, she had lived with them; she had also spent a good deal of time outside the convent walls. Who was she to start a Reform? By 1571, the convent of some 130 nuns was in desperate need of someone who could take things in hand. Because of this whole situation, the Apostolic Commissioner, Fray Pedro Fernandez, appointed Madre Teresa de Jesús prioress of the Encarnación.

Everyone expected trouble. Not only had Teresa been establishing convents of the Reform for several years, but she had also formally renounced the mitigated Rule in July 1571, and embraced the stricter rule of the Discalced. Furthermore, an outsider had appointed the prioress instead of the nuns electing her themselves as was usually done. The sisters, who were not interested in a stricter lifestyle and feared that Teresa would try to make them follow the Discalced Rule, opposed her nomination. Such issues did not make for a smooth transition of authority.

Despite this, on October 6, 1571, Fernandez remained firm in his decision and he named Teresa prioress. As expected, she encountered a good deal of resistance. On the day she was to take her place as prioress of the Encarnación, a small procession of people, including Madre Teresa de Jesús, Fray Angel de Salazar, the Provincial of the Calced Fathers, the Mayor of Avila, as well as some guards, walked northward along the city walls from the convent of San José in the eastern section of the city down the hill to the Encarnación. When they reached the convent and knocked at the doors, the nuns inside began shouting and screaming. They refused to let

Teresa enter and were not about to admit any of the others either. These nuns stridently hurled their insults at Teresa and adamantly rejected her as their new prioress. The more Fray Angel attempted to calm the nuns, the more determined they became. La Madre sat on a stone bench outside and waited. Finally, at one point, when Fray Angel pretended to leave, the shouting subsided long enough for a sister to cry out from within: "We want her!" Then while the door was opened, some of the nuns intoned the "Te Deum," creating further confusion among the sisters. The officials who had accompanied Teresa could still hear arguing within the cloister as they returned to the city. The sisters against having Teresa de Jesús as prioress still screamed at her and at their opponents. Those who favored Teresa shouted back. Gradually Teresa de Jesús transformed these violent beginnings into peace and calm.

The new prioress set about trying to put order into the convent. She obtained the appointment of Fray Juan de la Cruz as confessor to the sisters as soon as she reasonably could do so. She knew that his gentleness and deep knowledge of life with God would be most helpful to this convent. She also knew that his was not just intellectual knowledge, for she could see that he lived with God day by day. During the five years he spent at the Encarnación, he did in fact accomplish a great deal, though it is only human that not everyone within the convent was convinced of his wisdom.

There was a good deal of resistance, at least on the part of some sisters, to Fray Juan's appointment. While their greatest fears of being forced to follow the primitive Rule had not materialized, la Madre had made things more ordered and hence stricter. Now they regarded her naming of Fray Juan as their confessor just another subtle step toward making them a strict, contemplative group. They had been Calced and had always had the guidance of their own friars. Now Teresa intended to impose a Discalced friar upon them. To heighten their fears, this Fray Juan de la Cruz had a reputation for being very severe. Things were bound to be strained not only for the few days after his arrival but for several years.

La Madre's choice of Fray Juan de la Cruz as one of several confessors and guides in the spiritual life for the sisters of the Encarnación was a wise one indeed.[1] The nuns who suspected this appointment as a subtle edging toward the Reform were not totally wrong. Teresa wanted Fray Juan nearby so that they could easily discuss the Reform and more conveniently work out the difficulties involved. She also knew that with him as guide, all the sisters would gradually become more interested in deepening their spiritual life. Moreover, it was a fact that Teresa's activity in establishing Reform convents interested some of the nuns. All of these elements combined would make the convent much more faithful at least to the mitigated Rule of the Calced. However, none of this could be done without first instructing the sisters, theoretically and experientially, about the ideals of religious life in Carmel. Who better to do this than the little friar from Castile?

Fray Juan de la Cruz accepted this appointment with full awareness of its ramifications. Teresa had contacted the Apostolic Visitor, the Dominican Fray Pedro Fernandez, and had obtained the necessary permission and authorizations for the appointment of two friars chosen from among the Discalced: Fray Juan de la Cruz and Fray Germán de Santo Matía. This certainly did not help smooth matters over with the Calced Fathers of the Order. For years, the Calced had been the chaplains and confessors of the nuns at the Encarnación, and had been paid for their services. Now these two friars of the Reform came in with authorization of the Apostolic Visitor, and there was nothing that the Calced Friars could do but resign themselves to the facts. Some of the friars living at the Calced monastery on the hill were bitter. Jealousies, suspicions, and a dislike of the two friars abounded even before their arrival.

When Fray Juan and Fray Germán arrived during the summer of 1572, they lived at first with the Calced Friars at the Monastery of Nuestra Señora del Carmen. Located on the northern wall of the city, its bell tower was clearly visible from the monastery of the Encarnación, which lay just down the hill from the city walls. This meant that the friars who served as confessors and guides could easily reach the monastery by taking a short walk of perhaps five or ten minutes. While this was a physically convenient arrangement, the suspicions and hatred of some of the friars at the monastery caused Fray Juan and Fray Germán to move elsewhere in 1573.

On the property of the Encarnación, but outside the cloistered area, were several small huts near the monastery garden. These tiny buildings, right on the street and near one another, housed the families of the workmen employed by the monastery. Fray Juan and Fray Germán took up residence in one of these small huts. It was a poor place with hardly any furniture, but in keeping with the likes of the little friar in the coarse habit of the Discalced.

For the next four years, Fray Juan de la Cruz' life centered on Avila, this hut, and the monastery of the Encarnación.

Day after day he performed his usual routine tasks, but with a consciousness that made even little things seem different and important. During this period, he gradually came to see that what had seemed to be the height and final stage of his personal drama in Duruelo was only a first step in his new life. Fray Juan began each day in prayer with Fray Germán in their little house. Then Fray Juan would walk across the road to the monastery chapel to celebrate the Eucharist for the community there. Normally the sisters would go to confession every week or two. Thus, Fray Juan kept busy with this ministry alone. While this sacrament was not actually spiritual direction, Fray Juan's approach to it involved giving much encouragement and advice. He was too sensitive a man to use the sacrament of Reconciliation in a merely rote way. For him it was one of the meeting places between God and the human person. As such, it needed to be celebrated with patience, compassion, and understanding. When Fray Juan was involved, these qualities filled the sacrament because they were personal qualities he had received and nurtured within himself.

It was not long before many (though not all) of the nuns discovered what a marvelous guide they had in this man. Each sister related to him from her particular spiritual state at any given moment. The more serious the sisters were about their religious life, the more they saw in Fray Juan a man who could help them on their way to God. Often he would give the sisters who consulted him sayings written on small pieces of paper to serve as their guideposts. These points were similar to the actual *platicas* we find in his works such as: "Seek in reading and you will find in meditation; knock in prayer and it will be opened to you in contemplation."[2] "Take neither great nor little notice of who is with you or against you and try always to please God. Ask him that his will be done in you. Love him intensely, as he deserves to be loved."[3] "Be silent concerning what God may have given you and recall that saying of the bride: 'My secret for myself'" (Is 24:14).[4]

Through these maxims and other means, he tried to help the sisters to come to see that God was as real as the flowers in their garden. He wanted them to realize that this God touched their lives intimately, that they could find God within each person, in each life. The monastery had lost some of its sense of purpose, but Fray Juan, who had learned how to come closer to God, could offer light along the way to these nuns who searched for the real Center of their lives.

Fray Juan de la Cruz' actions showed the path to God and revealed God's presence in that path. Every day from the turnstile of the monastery, the nuns brought Fray Juan and Fray Germán's meals to their hut. Fray Juan ate whatever they sent without complaint. However, when he noticed that the cook had put something special on the tray, he would ask the sister to take it back to the monastery and give it to one of the sisters in the infirmary. This gesture was not motivated by an ascetical desire to punish his body but by his love for others. As always, the sick were the special objects of his love. He treated any gifts he received in the same way. He would give them to those who most needed them in order to bolster their spirits by demonstrating that someone really cared. His love for others was striking. By the age of thirty and onward, Fray Juan was already an incredibly gentle, sensitive, and compassionate human being.

One day as he was walking in the monastery, he saw a nun who was barefoot though she was not a member of the

Discalced Reform. She was not wearing shoes because the monastery did not have the money to buy her a pair. So Fray Juan went into the city of Avila to beg for money. When he had collected enough, he came back to the monastery and gave the money to the nun so she could buy a pair of shoes.

We cannot doubt that Fray Juan's attitude and activities were a result of his own life experiences in which God came to him, as the Creator comes to all human persons. Through the living out of his life, his consequent interaction with others, and his growing consciousness of God's presence, Fray Juan grew continuously into the man of God he was meant to be.

However, during this Avilan period, Fray Juan's work was not limited to the monastery. The hut he shared with Fray Germán was very close to the others occupied by the families of the workers. His hermitage sat in the midst of human life. Children played in the yards. Mothers shouted at them. Neighbors casually bantered across fences and in doorways. These families were as poor as his own had been in Fontiveros and Medina del Campo. Fray Juan had a deep interest and love for them all, for they were his kind of people. He played with the children and taught them the rudiments of reading and writing, as well as the catechism.[5] The children engaged him in conversation. These neighborly contacts made his life more ordinary, more rooted in day-to-day life than some might have thought. Years after his death, people remembered the kind and small friar who had lived near them at the Encarnación.

Through these neighbors and others who visited or saw Fray Juan occasionally in the narrow, busy streets of Avila, the people of the town came to know him. Certainly not everyone understood this friar in the rough habit, whose gaunt features gave a false impression of harshness and severity. Among those who had misconceptions about him was a rich young woman from the city. Her friends were concerned that her vain and selfish conduct would ruin her whole life. Yet, nothing they said seemed to have much influence on her. When they persisted in urging her to see Fray Juan at the monastery, she hesitated because he seemed so severe. She had all kinds of reasons why she should *not* go, but finally, because of the insistence of her friends, she gave in to their wishes and said that she would see Fray Juan.

As she walked down the hill to the monastery, the woman was still not convinced she should speak with Fray Juan. She felt deeply that he would not understand. Moreover, she believed he would make too many demands on her, demands that she knew she could never fulfill. These thoughts caused her to waver, but she struggled on to the monastery. Once in Fray Juan's presence, however, she realized how wrong she had been. As she told Fray Juan about her life, she began to feel more at ease. Then, to her surprise, when she had finished telling him her story, Fray Juan said that he would give her no other penance than what she had already suffered in coming to see him. Fray Juan realized how hard it had been for her to open her heart to him. He was becoming increasingly compassionate and insightful.

Fray Juan used his gifts wisely to give hope to people who thought there was nothing left to hope for in their lives. He would show them the positive dimensions of their lives and encourage them to live in the spirit of God's love. For example, one of the nuns told him of her terrible discouragement. Day after day, she reflected upon her life up to that point and how she had not been totally faithful to her vocation. She had become entangled in negative thinking and believed her sins so great that there was no hope for her. She was on the brink of despair. After revealing her innermost fears and thoughts, she looked at Fray Juan and waited anxiously in the silence. Fray Juan then spoke to her warmly of the God of love, who constantly forgives without question. This may have been the occasion for one of his more famous *platicas:* "When evening comes, you will be examined in love. Learn to love as God desires to be loved and abandon your own ways of acting."[6] Fray Juan's words produced an opening in her heart through which God's peace flooded her being. It was his personal conviction of God's love for everyone and everything that enabled Fray Juan de la Cruz to grow in his humanity and deep concern for others, no matter who they were or what their problems.

A second incident during Fray Juan's stay in Avila reveals another dimension of this unique individual. The event clearly impressed him, since he could still vividly recount it some twenty years later. It seems that his companion had gone away for a few days, so Fray Juan was alone in his little house. One evening, as he ate his meager supper, he heard someone coming through the small garden bordering his hut. As he turned from the table toward the door, he saw a beautiful young woman standing in the doorway. She lived in the city and he had seen her there, as well as at the monastery church. She was such a strikingly beautiful woman that anyone who laid eyes on her would have to notice. When she began to speak, the little friar found that her message surprised him much more than her presence. She passionately blurted out her desire to have him as her lover. It seems that she had fallen madly in love with him and wanted him to know it. Perhaps she thought he felt the same way. She acted with considerable daring for a woman of sixteenth-century Spain. Would he chase her out of the place as St. Thomas Aquinas is said to have done in similar circumstances? Would he shout and scream condemnation at her for such sinful brazenness? Would he perhaps accede to her passion? In fact, he responded in none of these ways. Instead, they spoke together. What Fray Juan said to her that evening no one knows, but afterward she went back to her home on the hill in Avila understanding the impossibility of the kind of relationship she had desired with him. Fray Juan had spoken to her calmly and gently because this was his manner of acting. Years before he had vowed to be faithful to God and to his fellow Carmelites. And once Fray Juan had made a commitment, he remained loyal as long as he lived. He persevered even when fidelity caused him personal difficulty and pain. This young woman saw that the friar she loved had chosen God fully. What she did not know, however, was how Fray Juan felt as he spoke those calming words to her.

When he narrated this story to his friend, Fray Juan Evangelista, in the last years of his life, Fray Juan de la Cruz told him how utterly appealing he had found this young woman. He had been very attracted to her in every way.[7] This story reveals to us a man, a human being who was able to live within his own flesh, committed to the One whom he had chosen years earlier, no matter what the circumstances. However, this was no more a simple thing for him than for any other person. Passions, desires, mortality, human circumstances are the stuff in which commitment takes root and grows. Fray

Juan became the deeply human person he was not by denying this life and all that it comprises. He grew by acknowledging and living his life more and more consciously. It was not easy, but he tried continuously, and, like all human persons, no doubt he failed as he struggled along the way to God.

Because he too had feelings and passions, he was able to help others through painful periods in their lives. While he was in Avila, a nun was deeply, passionately involved with a man in the city. After a while, her behavior and her inability to change troubled her immensely. After speaking with Fray Juan, she finally renewed her original commitment to God, which infuriated her lover. Moreover, he knew that the one to blame for her change of attitude was the young confessor of the Encarnación. The man was not about to let that little friar get away with such a thing. One evening, after Fray Juan had heard the sisters' confessions, he began to walk back to his nearby hut. Suddenly someone burst out of the shadows and beat him severely. Still swollen and bruised a few days later, Fray Juan refused to say who had attacked him. He would only say that it was right that he should suffer in his service of God. He also wanted to save the man and nun from public ridicule. He was indeed an amazingly sensitive and faithful man.

While living at the Encarnación, Fray Juan de la Cruz would occasionally be called upon to travel to other convents where he was needed for one reason or another. He made one of these visits in response to an appeal to exorcise a nun in Medina del Campo. After meeting the nun, he told her superiors that she was not possessed, but simply suffering from a mental illness. In an age when fear of possession and of evil spirits abounded, it took a very balanced and insightful person to see clearly and steer people away from supernatural explanations of purely natural maladies.

During this visit to Medina del Campo, Fray Juan visited his mother and brother. He loved them very much, and would certainly not have gone to this city without stopping to spend at least a little time with them.[8] No doubt he spoke with his mother about his life with the Discalced Friars and of his happiness despite the difficulties the community was encountering.

The events of another trip reveal the frustration the Discalced Carmelites endured as they tried to establish new houses. In mid-March 1574, Fray Juan went with Madre Teresa de Jesús, Fray Julian de Avila, and a few others to establish a convent in Segovia. Though they did not have the written permission of the bishop, he had nonetheless told them they could open a monastery of Discalced Carmelite nuns. This they planned to do on March 19, 1574, the feast of St. Joseph. However, the bishop was away when they arrived in Segovia. La Madre instinctively feared that the Vicar General would object to their establishing the monastery without the bishop's written authorization. Consequently, Teresa arranged to have Fray Julian de Avila celebrate Eucharist early in the morning and for Fray Juan to celebrate a later second Eucharist. According to the custom of the time, this would automatically establish the monastery and nothing could be done to change it. (Teresa tended to use a variety of ruses when she did not have all of the necessary papers and authorizations.) However, matters did not go as smoothly as she had hoped.

When the Vicar General heard about the early morning events that took place just a short walk from the cathedral, he was understandably furious. He charged down the slight incline toward the monastery and made such a din upon arriving that Fray Julian ran and hid, while Madre Teresa and Fray Juan were left alone to greet the angry diocesan official. He shouted his orders: "The Blessed Sacrament is to be consumed. The decorations of this so-called chapel are to be removed, and a guard will be placed at the door to prevent any further Eucharistic celebrations." He even threatened to put Fray Juan de la Cruz in jail for helping to establish the monastery within the Segovian jurisdiction. Despite the threats, Fray Juan remained calm. La Madre tried to explain the situation to the Vicar General, who was really no match for her—she was never one to give in quickly or easily. The affair was settled after a few days and soon the small monastery was well on its way to taking root in the beautiful, ancient Roman city of Spain.

During his week in Segovia, Fray Juan took the opportunity to walk through the woods just outside the city where he could be alone to reflect and pray. As he progressed down the steepening slope of Segovia toward the Alcazar palace where Isabella had been crowned queen almost 100 years earlier, he sensed that one day he would return. Past the palace towers, which pierced the bright blue Segovian sky far below the steep cliff, he saw the glittering waters of the Eresma River wending its way around the rocky precipice upon which the palace was built. It looked like a huge Spanish galleon sailing into the infinite blue space. He could still hear the waters from the river gurgling and rushing through the valley as he climbed the opposite hillside where flocks of sheep usually grazed during the summer months. Still cold in mid-March, patches of snow remained here and there on the ground. However, it was easy for Fray Juan to image the pastoral scene of summer. The natural beauty of the Segovian countryside impressed itself upon his mind and imagination. Fray Juan's sensitivity to nature's beauty stored these sights in his memory, where they rested until he would someday call them forth in his poetry.

Rising Tension

Fray Juan de la Cruz matured during his time in Avila. While other friars and nuns busily established Discalced Carmelite monasteries for men, and some for women, he kept to his more restricted work of administering the sacraments for the sisters at the Encarnación, teaching the children who lived nearby, and giving spiritual guidance to various people. Though he fasted as the Rule directed and lived his vow of poverty in an authentic way, he no longer indulged in the extreme ascetical practices of earlier years. He attempted to develop his sense of prayer, his consciousness of God's continual presence within him and in the world around him. When he was not actively ministering to the nuns or the people of the city, he would write snippets of poetry or carve figures of Christ crucified or other objects which would remind him of God's coming to live with God's people.

After many months of prayer and reflection, Fray Juan had a unique insight into the crushing agony of Jesus on the cross. His penetration into the mystery of Jesus' own suffering and every human person's own relationship to it inspired Fray Juan to render a unique sketch of the crucifixion. The three-inch-long sketch can be seen today in a reliquary at the

monastery of the Encarnación. In this sketch of Christ crucified, the view is from above, the body is weighed down,
drooping earthward. Blood drips from Christ's hands and
head. One sees a broken body, lifeless yet life-giving. This is
what Fray Juan saw in his own heart. This is what he felt. This
insight into Christ's own life-producing suffering and death
was certainly a grace, which would serve him well in the coming months.

The Reform Teresa de Jesús had started was now beginning to cause serious problems. Various factions arose because
of the Reform group, and this slowly began to divide the
Carmelite family. Some Carmelites disliked what was happening, and others felt that those wanting to live according to the
stricter Rule were getting too strong. Still others were jealous.
However, the difficulties that grew daily cannot be attributed
entirely to those who did not wish to follow the primitive
Rule. The Discalced group did contain some very strong and
even obnoxious personalities. Some of Teresa's own means of
establishing the Reform were at times suspicious if not devi-
ous. A serious conflict was to be expected, and, interestingly
enough, what brought the issue to a head came through the
actions of people who were not even Carmelites.

Because of a request of Felipe II, a Brief from Rome
was obtained appointing two Dominicans as Apostolic Commissioners: Fray Francisco de Vargas and Fray Pedro
Fernandez, one for the northern part of Spain (New and Old
Castile) and one for the southern part (Andalusia). Their
appointment conferred upon them great power over the
Carmelite Order. Fray Francisco de Vargas, the Commissioner
for Andalusia, was not as sensitive a person as Fray Pedro

Fernandez, the Commissioner for Castile. Fernandez worked closely with the different friars involved, while Vargas simply forced issues. For example, Vargas took a house in Huelva from the Calced Friars and gave it to the Discalced. Then he authorized the foundation of houses in Sevilla, Granada, and La Peñuela for the Discalced, despite the fact that the Carmelite Superior General, Padre Rubeo, had expressly forbidden setting up houses of the Reform in Andalusia.

Naturally, these actions aroused great fear among many members of the Calced Carmelites. Therefore, in early 1574, the Calced Carmelites decided to send representatives to Rome seeking to cancel the powers given to the Apostolic Commissioners. By August 3, 1574, the representatives were in possession of a papal document which revoked the Commissioners' rather wide-sweeping powers. However, when the Papal Nuncio, Ormaneto, heard of this document, he used his authority as the pope's representative to reappoint Fernandez and Vargas on December 27, 1574, and gave them even greater power. The Calced Carmelites were understandably angry. The Reform seemed like total rebellion to them. They decided to discuss the whole matter at the General Chapter, whose decisions would be binding upon the whole Order, as it met in May of 1575 at Piacenza, Italy.

Meanwhile, the Superior General, Padre Rubeo, wrote to Madre Teresa asking for an explanation of what was happening. Unfortunately, she did not receive the letter until June of 1575, a month after the Chapter had deliberated on the problem. Unaware that Teresa had not received the Superior General's letter, the members of the Chapter attributed her lack of response to her headstrong and rebellious character.

As part of the corrective measures the Chapter wanted to establish, it appointed a special Visitor for Spain and Portugal. Padre Jeronimo Tostado seemed the perfect man for the position. He had arrived in Spain by mid-1576, but the conflict between his papers and the orders of the Papal Legate led the Royal Council to refuse him the necessary permission to fulfill his mandate. Tostado then left for Portugal to work there until the matter of permissions was settled.

In the meantime, the Discalced Friars called for a meeting to begin on September 9, 1576 at Almodovar del Campo. The purpose of the meeting was to discuss the two emerging tendencies in lifestyle within the Discalced communities: one toward contemplative living, and the other toward more apostolic living. After a long debate, during which Fray Juan de la Cruz defended the more contemplative lifestyle, the group chose to stress the apostolic dimension. With this question settled, they then turned their attention to their relationship with the Calced Friars. The Discalced made a real attempt to pacify the Calced Friars, and among their decisions was the removal of Fray Juan from his position as confessor at the Encarnación. The friars felt that this action would alleviate some of the friction between the Calced and themselves. (However, either because the nuns intervened or because the Papal Nuncio reappointed Fray Juan, he continued working at the Encarnación.) Despite their good intentions, the problems between the two groups did not come to an immediate resolution. In fact, ultimately only a complete separation would take care of most of these problems.

Even before the meeting in 1576, the situation had deteriorated to such an extent that in early 1576 the first public

arrest of Fray Juan took place. The prior of the Calced Friars of
Avila publicly removed Fray Juan de la Cruz and his companion from their hermitage and took them as prisoners to the
monastery at Medina del Campo, where Fray Juan had been a
novice. The Calced Friars not only felt they were in a strong
enough position to do this, but they believed their actions were
perfectly justified. What they had not realized was the popular
support Fray Juan had behind him because of his ministry to
the people of the area. When the people of Avila heard about
his arrest, they became very angry and sought the intervention
of the Papal Legate, Ormaneto, and he ordered the immediate
release of Fray Juan de la Cruz. Furthermore, he forbade any
Calced friar from serving in any capacity at the monastery of
the Encarnación. (Up to this time, some Calced Friars still
acted as the sisters' confessors.) The Calced Friars had to obey,
yet the resentment they harbored in their hearts warned that
the battle was not over. Ormaneto's actions assured that the differences between the two groups would continue.

Fray Juan was not directly involved in all the disputes, but
he had a certain reputation, which made him the particular
object of the Calced Friars' efforts to stop the Reform. The
disputes and the direction the Discalced group was taking
took its toll on Fray Juan. He appeared thinner than usual. He
was very tired. His face was drawn. He continued to perform
his ministry as if nothing was happening, and except for his
physical appearance, he was very much the same.

Those who saw Fray Juan did not realize the heavy bur-
dens he carried. He was so sensitive that the animosity and
bitterness he saw and felt around him caused him to suffer
greatly. His insight into Jesus' suffering on the cross was born

of his own crushing pain at seeing the ongoing battles among his brothers. Things had changed from the early, peaceful days at Duruelo just some eight years before. And the difficulties were not over yet.

Ormaneto, who had been so favorable to the Discalced Friars, died on June 18, 1577. He would no longer be there to protect the leaders of the Reform with his papal authority. The gates were now open to the opponents of the Discalced Carmelites, and the Calced Friars, who now viewed the whole Reform movement as revolutionary and rebellious, lost no time in bringing it to its knees. Perhaps some of the Calced friars may have considered the Reform good and sincere, but most saw its dangers and the obstinacy of its members. And they too were sincere, honest men. For the good of the Church, for peace and order, they thought it best to control or perhaps stop this new movement entirely. The appointment of Filippo Sega as the new Papal Legate confirmed their point of view. Before leaving Rome, Sega had already spoken with the Calced superiors in the Eternal City and, therefore, was not favorably disposed toward the Discalced.

It was in this atmosphere that the Calced Friars performed their most daring act, which inaugurated the most influential period in the life of Fray Juan de la Cruz.

CHAPTER IV

The Dark Night of Imprisonment in Toledo
(1577–1578)

THE DRAWING TO A CLOSE OF THE YEAR 1577 was a welcomed event for Fray Juan. The pressure from the Calced Friars was increasing day by day as they sought to control, if not end, the Reform movement. The new Papal Legate, Filippo Sega, proved more antagonistic toward these "rebellious friars." Though the decrees of the Council of Piacenza, held two years earlier, were still partially held in abeyance, they hung over both Calced and Discalced Carmelites like a cloud of foreboding. Even life at the Encarnación had been terribly disturbed. In December, some of the nuns were still under excommunication because they had insisted on having Madre Teresa de Jesús as their prioress instead of the woman named by the authorities. Tension was growing and Fray Juan de la Cruz felt it too. As a result, his frailty became even more evident. He was exhausted, but he was not about to have a rest.

When the Chapter gave orders to reduce or simply contain the growth of the Discalced Friars, Fray Juan seemed to pay no heed. If he did not actively and personally countermand the orders of the Superior General and the Chapter, he certainly seemed to go along with the actions of the Discalced. His silence was perceived as approval. His continued discussions with Madre Teresa implicated him in the revolt. The Calced Friars thought he was behind all the difficulties. The little friar who had once been one of them was now blatantly disobedient, and he was not simply disobeying a few minor rules. He was defying the highest authority in the Order. Could this friar be another Martin Luther, whom most Spaniards thought was determined to cause the Church so many problems? If so, then they had to stop him immediately. The vow of obedience was a keystone of religious life, and this Juan de la Cruz was breaking it down too openly. For the Calced Friars, he was simply a defiant rebel. In his stubborn pride, he would destroy the Order and perhaps lead the Church in Spain down the road to rebellion and even heresy. They had to stop the Reform. The Calced Friars drew up a plan. They would pounce on the leaders of the Reform and toss them into prison, halt the movement's growth, and, by these harsh measures, perhaps succeed in bringing the irksome revolutionaries to repent of their folly. They intended to execute their plan swiftly, before the end of 1577.

The winter had already set in on the Avilan plain. The mountains in the distance, now covered in snow, seemed to be slowly spreading their white blanket toward the city of Avila. In their tiny hut, Fray Juan de la Cruz and Fray Germán de Santo Matía tried to keep warm. The bitter winds and frost had already turned the ground outside brittle and hard. They had both suffered the piercing cold that December day going to the monastery several times for the Eucharist and other functions. Though the monastery was only a short walk away, Fray Juan had felt the intense cold cutting through him and his thin body shivered. Even his rather heavy, rough habit had not protected him from the cold wind that also bit at his bare feet. The sun had gone down early on that December 2, 1577, as the two men, somewhat protected from the elements, settled down for the night.

As the two friars prayed together before retiring, they heard the frozen ground crunching under the footsteps that hurried down the hill toward their hut. The friars would soon discover that a group of Calced friars, police, and citizens was coming to kidnap them.

When the group reached the door, they broke it open and, as they rushed inside, there was a good deal of noise and confusion. Though neither Fray Juan nor Fray Germán resisted, they were handled roughly and one of them bled from the mouth. The small group dragged the friars out of the hut and quickly pushed them up the hill to the Calced monastery. The gang feared that the noise might attract attention and they wanted to hide their prisoners as quickly as possible to avoid complications. The orders of Fray Jeronimo Tostado, the Vicar General of the Order, were fulfilled; the two friars were now safely in the hands of the Calced Friars.

Once in the monastery, the prisoners were forced to remove the rough habits of the Reform and put on the more refined habits of the Calced Friars. Then both were whipped twice and put into monastic cells. The following morning, when Fray Juan was freed in order to celebrate the Eucharist, he used this opportunity to escape. He ran down the steep hill to his hut in order to destroy some letters and documents, which would have hurt the Reform if they had fallen into the hands of the Calced Friars. His captors quickly discovered his escape and ran down the hill after Fray Juan. By the time they arrived at the hut, he had almost finished destroying the documents. He had just enough time to destroy the last papers as they pounded violently on the door he had bolted.

Fearing Fray Juan might escape again or that the people of the city would come to rescue him and Fray Germán, the Calced Friars decided to transfer them elsewhere. They sent Fray Germán to the Monastery of San Pablo de la Moraleja that is located between Avila and Medina del Campo, and they took Fray Juan de la Cruz to Toledo.

It did not take long for the nuns of the Encarnación to realize what had happened. Though they had not understood what was going on, several had heard the violent sounds coming from the direction of the huts the night of Fray Juan's arrest. Once they had discovered the truth, the sisters immediately informed la Madre. She was terribly upset. On December 4, 1577, she wrote a letter to King Felipe II of Spain who was then in Madrid.[1] In her letter, she wrote of what had happened and gave some of the background. Then she said:

> I feel very sad to see confessors in the hands of those friars [Calced] who for some days have been desiring to seize hold of them. I would consider the confessors better off if they were held by the Moors, who perhaps would show more compassion. And this one friar [Fray Juan de la Cruz], who is so great a servant of God, is so weak from all that he has suffered that I fear for his life.[2]

This and the other letters she wrote so furiously came to nothing. The king probably avoided becoming involved in the issue because disobedience in religious communities was often handled in this way. At any rate, while not forgotten, no one could effectively help Fray Juan. This suffering was his and his alone to bear. It was to be painful—even beyond imagining—but it was also to be *the* most significant growth-experience of his life.

The long trek to Toledo was not easy. The Calced Friars did not want to take him by the most direct route for fear that their prisoner might be recognized if they passed through major towns and cities along the way. They decided instead to go through the Sierra Guadarrama, as sleet and snow pounded on them. Aside from the severe weather, Fray Juan also had to bear the jibes and taunts of his captors. The days seemed terribly long and the journey endless. When they finally approached Toledo, Fray Juan was exhausted, cold, and wet. To keep him from knowing exactly where he was, his captors had blindfolded him and doubled back and forth on their tracks as they brought him into the city late at night.

Toledo

The incredibly beautiful imperial city of Toledo, some seventy kilometers south of Madrid, rests on a hill above the Tagus River that flows around the city, protecting it like a moat. Ancient walls and the cathedral dominate its skyline. Inside the walls, one is in the midst of a series of calm squares and steep, narrow cobblestone walkways. In the winter, the stone walls of the majestic buildings hold off the cold sharp winds. In the summer, a stifling heat burns the ancient stones as the sun pounds the pavement. Toledo is a mystic city as can be seen in a painting by El Greco, who arrived there the very year of Fray Juan de la Cruz' imprisonment in 1577.

However, Fray Juan would not see the city's beauty; his view would be severely limited. The Toledo monastery of the Calced Friars was one of the most striking in Spain. A very large building, it housed some eighty friars quite comfortably. Yet within this rambling cloister, Fray Juan lived in a space hardly suitable even for storage.

After throwing him into a monastic cell, the friars shortly thereafter transferred him to another "cell," which in fact was only the closet of an adjoining guest room. The "closet" was only six feet wide and ten feet long; it had a solid wood door and no window to let in any light. The only illumination came from a two-inch-wide opening high up in the wall separating the room from a hallway. In order for Fray Juan to read his breviary—the only book he was allowed to keep—he had to stand and hold it up to catch the faint rays of light that managed to filter in. Even so, it was very hard on his eyes, but at least he managed to read his Office.

His first minutes in this cell were terrifying. He stumbled across something on the floor. As his eyes adjusted to the darkness, he could see more. With his hands extended before him, he found what was to be his bed: a few boards on the floor and an old blanket or two that offered little protection from the wintry dampness of the cold stone floors and walls. A bucket sat in the corner. This was to be his toilet. Situated quite near the monastery toilets, the room already had a very unpleasant smell. This dark and smelly "prison" would be his home for several months. In fact, it would be a place of physical and spiritual darkness, anguish, and pain. The conditions in which the friars kept Fray Juan wore him down slowly but surely. The food was minimal and always the same thing: a few scraps left over from the Carmelite table. As time went on, he became weaker, more fatigued, and paranoid. He became more and more certain that the friars were trying to kill him, as seen in his reaction to the few sardines he occasionally received as part of his meal. Sardines were relatively rare, and, as a result, this heightened his suspicion that they were poisoned. His fear was so strong that each bit he ate required a special effort. And as he would eat these sardines, he would attempt to distract himself by forgiving his imagined killers. The lack of proper food weakened him considerably, yet he was forced to undergo a particularly painful and scarring ceremony.

Every Friday the friars dragged Fray Juan to the common dining room where he was given bread and water—his sole sustenance for that day. As the other friars ate their food at tables located along the walls of the large refectory, Fray Juan ate his bread kneeling in the very center of the room on the stone floor. Once the superior finished eating, he would begin to harangue Fray Juan in the presence of all the brothers.

"You, Juan de la Cruz, are but a rebellious, stubborn man who desires nothing but your own fame and honor. In your hardheadedness you are destroying all that is good in Holy Mother Church and our own community of Carmel. At a time when our Mother Church is being besieged by even more destructive forces from without, you, Juan, weaken it from within. You refuse to obey. Obedience, that faithful cornerstone of religious life, is treated by you as simply trash to be trampled underfoot. The General Chapter of Piacenza ordered all you contemplatives not to establish new houses, not to wear a different habit, not to accept novices. But you persist in your own satanically inspired ways. Disregarding the commands of the General or the Chapter and even the orders of the representative of our Holy Father the Pope, you scandalize our holy Order. You scandalize the people of our Holy

Mother the Church. In all your stubbornness, you weaken the faith of all believers. How can you maintain your satanic stance in the face of such horrors you are causing? Repent of your disobedience. We will forgive you and take you back into our very hearts. Work now with us to preserve the faith in this world that is so possessed by Satan and his cohorts. Repent of your disobedience. We only ask that you exercise your vow and the virtue of obedience and simply follow the commands of the Legate, your superiors, and the General Chapter. Admit your disobedience and follow the orders of your Church, and once again you will serve Holy Mother Church, as she deserves to be served."

Friday after Friday (and even more often at the beginning of his imprisonment), these or similar words rang out and echoed down the stone chamber near the monastery dining room. How strange and painful these words must have sounded, coming to him as they did from good, sincere men: his fellow Carmelites. What had he done that would cause them to regard him this way? Were they really talking about him? Was he not simply following the orders of the higher authority, the former Legate? Was the Reform as evil as his superior insisted? The questions pressed upon him more strongly as he heard these rebukes time and time again.

While the final words of the superior still rang in Fray Juan's ears, all the friars would stand. One by one, they would approach him as in unison they chanted the *Miserere*. First the prior and then each of the friars would whip the bared shoulders of the little revolutionary with a short, knotted triple rope that bit into his flesh time after time. The friars who believed him most guilty put all their force into their one blow. Others, who believed that they were treating Fray Juan too harshly, felt the sting in their own hearts and bodies, and they struck him as gently as they could. By the time he was led back to his wintry hole in the wall, the blood from his wounds would trickle from his shoulders and back.

As days lengthened into weeks, and weeks into months, conditions worsened. The friars tempted Fray Juan with promises to make him a superior of any Calced monastery he might want if only he would obey them. They even promised to give him a gold crucifix. (How little they knew the man!) These bribes did not affect him, but their words of rebuke and correction did. "Maybe I am wrong," he thought. "Perhaps they are right. After all, I owe my obedience to my religious superiors, and these men are my superiors. Am I to suffer all of this simply to be sent to hell for my evil, recalcitrant ways? Am I to be separated from my God and my beloved Church for no reason at all? Am I serving the demons themselves?" He reached the point where he was no longer so sure of his position.

Fray Juan's imprisonment in the cold, foul-smelling, and moldy cell and his poor diet took their toll. His appetite was failing—some days he simply could not eat at all—and he kept losing weight. This and the little sleep he got, as well as the lack of light, so affected him that he began to suffer from dysentery. Some days his guard did not even allow him to empty his bucket, and this intensified the foul odor in his cell. Yet, even this was not enough for his captors.

The friars persisted in their attempts to break his fidelity to the Reform. They would talk outside his cell about how all the others involved in the Reform had already surrendered and returned to the Calced Carmelites. Sometimes they would loudly suggest that they could throw Fray Juan into an empty well outside the city and no one would be the wiser. From their exaggerated statements, made for his benefit, Fray Juan de la Cruz received greatly distorted ideas of what was actually happening. Everyone else—including the leaders of the Discalced—seemed to have given up. What reason was there for him to remain firm? Fray Juan was confused and doubted the reasonableness of continuing to resist. He had reached the point where he wished God would let him die. In fact, he prayed for this.

He would not find such release, however. Instead, in addition to all of his physical pain and mental doubt, there came an even more terrifying element. Until then, God had been the one steadfast part of his life. From his early years at the Hospital de Las Bubas in Medina del Campo and throughout his days as a Carmelite in the city and in Salamanca, Fray Juan had always felt the reality of God's presence. This had been wonderfully intensified during his days in Duruelo— those idyllic months when God seemed so real and so close. Even the spiritual joys he experienced at the Encarnación seemed to pale in the light of Duruelo. Despite the hardships during the first months of his imprisonment in Toledo, he could still always pray and somehow know God to be present.

Now things changed radically. Fray Juan suffered the complete absence of God, but not just the light, momentary absence most believers experience. The absence was total. It seemed to Fray Juan that his entire life, past and present, was wasted. He could no longer pray. The very thought of God made him physically sick. He felt abandoned in his degradation. He was terribly ill. His underclothes were literally rotting away on his body. The man who was so meticulous about personal cleanliness had not been able to wash for months. And as the summer approached with its stifling, unbearable, scorching heat, his closet cell became an oven. In his suffering how could Fray Juan not cry out from his heart: "Where is this cursed God? Why am I here? Why? Why?"

Many years later Fray Juan de la Cruz would seem to be recalling this experience when he described the purifying flame of God and observed that

> ...a person suffers great deprivation and feels heavy afflictions in the spirit that ordinarily overflow into the senses, for this flame is extremely oppressive. In this preparatory purgation the flame is not bright for a person, but dark.... It is not gentle, but afflictive. Even though it sometimes imparts the warmth of love, it does so with torment and pain. And it is not delightful,... but it is consuming and contentious, making a person faint and suffer with self-knowledge. Thus it is not glorious for the soul, but rather makes it feel wretched and distressed in the spiritual light of self-knowledge which it bestows.... At this stage a person suffers from sharp trials in the intellect, severe dryness and distress in the will, and from the burdensome knowledge of their own miseries in the memory, for their spiritual eye gives them a very clear picture of themselves. In the substance of the soul they suffer abandonment, supreme poverty, dryness, cold, and sometimes heat. They find relief in nothing, nor does any thought console them, nor can they even raise the heart to God, so oppressed are they by this flame.... For when the soul suffers all these things jointly, it truly seems that God has become displeased with it and cruel.[3]

Such spiritual pain and anguish simply cannot be narrated; Fray Juan was crushed, destroyed. Unable to rise from the pit of his darkness, he languished alone, desperately alone, and cried out from the depths of his agonized soul. All seemed for nothing. Then, to add to his troubles, he experienced strong passions and desires, things he had never imagined existed within him, or that he thought he had suppressed years ago. These passions and desires kept coming back to his consciousness again and again, and his sensitivity and imaginative ability heightened their visual intensity. Everything seemed to be dragging him further down, plunging him into absolute darkness. He could do nothing but suffer seeing it all and himself. This physical and spiritual onslaught continued unrelentingly for weeks. He lived it in crushing anguish. No one spoke to him and he spoke to no one. It was his ordeal to bear and live.

The exact duration of this horrible trial is unknown, but by May 1578, he had passed through the worst of it and had been remade. His life of belief had reached a new stage; he had survived and grown. Now he knew he could find God not only in light, but in darkness as well. His experience became the basic pattern for his description of the soul's dark nights on its way to God.

Escape

In the spring of 1578, a new jailer, Fray Juan de Santa María, was assigned to guard Fray Juan de la Cruz. For months before this appointment, Fray Juan de Santa María had seen how badly the others had treated the prisoner. It was not very long before his close contact enabled him to know Fray Juan as he really was: kind, gentle, patient, even-tempered, and faithful. Moreover, he saw how desperately the captive friar needed some change. He began by providing Fray Juan with a clean, new tunic to replace the one he had been wearing since his imprisonment began. Then came a totally unexpected gift. While the other friars took their daily siesta, Fray Juan de Santa María would unlock the door of Fray Juan's cell and let him roam outside to get some light and fresh air. Fray Juan was so appreciative that he thanked the jailer profusely and gave him the small wooden crucifix with a bronze corpus that he had worn under his tunic near his heart. Their relationship developed so well that Fray Juan de la Cruz risked asking his guard for some paper, pen, and ink for writing. There was no hesitation in his guard's mind and soul; he gave Fray Juan the materials he had so longed for.

In an effort to keep his mind alert, and hence himself alive, Fray Juan began composing poems. His imagination allowed him to break out of his stultifying prison and roam the countryside. He remembered Segovia's northern and southern winds blowing over the flat fields just above the silver rush of the Eresma River surrounding the cliffs on which the Alcazar is built. In his mind's eye he traveled through luscious woodlands and grazing fields, touching and smelling all their beauty. He found lovers, passionate and full of desire and love. He remembered the parts of Scripture he loved so much: the Song of Songs and the various psalms. Now, in this dark, dank jail, he wrote down some of what he had already composed in his mind: the first thirty-one stanzas of *The Spiritual Canticle*, the *Song of the Soul that Rejoices in Knowing God Through Faith*, the *Romance Poems on the Gospel "In Principio erat Verbum,"* and *A Romance on the Psalm "By the Waters of Babylon"*

(Ps 136). With great care he set them down on the paper and kept them close by. These poems contained his inner anguish and beauty. They expressed the process that was forming and had formed him.

He captured his suffering when he wrote:

> By the rivers of Babylon I sat down weeping, there on the ground and remembering you, O Zion, whom I loved, in that sweet memory I wept even more.... I died within myself for you and for you I revived, because the memory of you gave life and took it away. The strangers among whom I was captive rejoiced; they asked me to sing what I sang in Zion: Sing us a song from Zion, let's hear how it sounds. I said: How can I sing, in a strange land where I weep for Zion, sing of the happiness that I had there?[4]

The more famous *The Spiritual Canticle* speaks of the desire for the Beloved whom he had come to know so deeply in his imprisonment. While composing and recomposing these works, he kept himself sane. Yet, his physical condition continued to deteriorate. He was dying day by day. As the summer heat worsened, he could hardly bear it, and he feared for his survival. All the pain he had experienced was still there, but it no longer controlled him. He had broken through, and, despite the continuing ordeal, he could live and grow.

Weakened and tortured, he knew he had to do something. Shortly before the feast of the Assumption, an unexpected visit became the catalyst for a decision. That day, when his cell door opened, the superior and two friars entered. Fray Juan de la Cruz remained hunched over on the floor in their presence. The superior became terribly annoyed that Juan had not moved, so he kicked him and said, "Why don't you rise when your superior comes in?"[5] With great effort, the tired little friar got up and excused himself. He had not risen because of his physical condition and he had mistaken them for the jailer. Then Fray Juan courageously asked if he could celebrate the Eucharist the next day on the feast of the Assumption. The superior's answer was rapid and stunning: "Not in my lifetime you won't." With that, one of the friars said to the superior, "Come, Father, let's leave this hovel. It's too foul smelling."[6] The door slammed shut behind them and, as the key turned in the lock, a decision unlocked within Fray Juan. Escape was the only route left open to him.

When his new jailer had eased his restrictions, Fray Juan began familiarizing himself with the section of the monastery where his cell was located. The adjoining room and the hallway with its observation window and small balcony provided a view of the city wall some twelve or so feet below and the Tagus River at the foot of the rocky cliffs.

Now determined to escape, Fray Juan studied his surroundings more carefully. One day he tried to measure the distance from the window to the wall. Taking some thread he had been given to sew his tattered habit, he weighted it with a small rock and lowered it from the window. With this rough measurement, and taking into account his own height, he determined that he might just be able to fall a short distance on to the wall. An escape seemed possible, but there were many questions to consider. Would he wake someone and be caught if he tried to escape at night? How would he get the lock off the door? What would he use for a rope to climb down the window? Was it really possible? But Fray Juan simply could not wait any longer; he had to take a chance.

He began to seriously plan his move. Each day when he went out for his walk, he loosened the screws of the lock on his door, removing and replacing them right up to the day of his escape. The screws were loose enough so that he would simply have to push the door and the lock would fall off. The friars' rooms were far enough away so that the noise of the lock falling to the floor would not arouse them. The day of his escape, Fray Juan tore his blankets into strips and sewed them together to make a twelve-foot rope. Then he took the handle of a candle lamp and attached it to one end of the rope. It would act as a hook to hold his rope to the balcony. Everything seemed ready. He spent his time outside during the siesta going over the details of his escape. When the jailer brought him back to his cell, he did not notice the loosened screws. Fray Juan waited for nightfall, feeling somewhat apprehensive but determined.

Then a new wrinkle developed that threatened to destroy his plans. Two visiting friars arrived at the monastery later that day, and the friars gave them the room adjoining Fray Juan's cell. It was a very hot night and the friars kept their door open to let more air into the room. They also moved their beds onto the floor near the door where it was a bit cooler. Unfortunately, they did not retire early, but talked for some time. Meanwhile, Fray Juan struggled with his decision. Should he postpone his escape attempt? Would another time be better? In the end, he decided to proceed as planned.

Around two o'clock in the morning, when all seemed quiet, Fray Juan pushed firmly on the door of his cell and the lock fell to the floor with such a noise it seemed like the burst of cannon to him. The visiting friars awoke and shouted,

"Who's there?" Fray Juan stood still though his heart pounded within him as if it would burst. He held his breath wondering if the friars would get up, but they must have concluded that the noise came from outside and went back to sleep.

In the darkness, Fray Juan could only make out the shadows of the men lying on the floor. He stepped carefully around them. Once outside the door, he walked quickly to the balcony window with his makeshift rope in hand. He attached the lamp handle to the wooden railing, then he took his habit off and threw it onto the wall below. He started lowering himself down the rope. The wooden railing gave a little, but it held. When he reached the end of the rope, he realized he would have to swing a little in order to fall directly onto the wall that was less than two feet wide. Inadvertently some workmen had increased the danger by loosening the top stones to prepare for repairs the following day. If Fray Juan missed the wall and fell on the other side, he would be killed on the jagged cliffs descending into the Tagus River below. Fully aware of this danger, yet determined to proceed, he let go and fell safely on the top of the wall. He put on his habit and went on.

Now he had to find a way off the wall and into the city. The only thought that raced through his mind was that he must find the Discalced Carmelite nuns of Toledo. They would help him; he was sure of that. He moved cautiously along the wall. The moon provided a little light and he saw what he thought was an alleyway. He lowered himself down and discovered to his dismay that he was in the garden of a nearby convent of nuns. If he were caught there, it would mean a terrible scandal and he would be back in jail under even stricter surveillance. He frantically rushed around looking for a way out, but the walls were too high for him to scale, especially in his weakened condition. His heart beat more rapidly in panic. His breathing became heavier. He perspired profusely and his whole body felt racked by pain. Then, in a sudden burst of energy, he climbed out of the garden by the corner of the wall.

Once more on top of the wall, he walked along and went down into what he now felt certain was a street. It was still dark, but sunrise was not far off. Suddenly, seeing him a woman called out, "Fray, it is too dark to be outside. Come and spend the night with me." He walked on more quickly. Others who had been nearby and heard the woman ridiculed Fray Juan and called after him. He began to run until he could run no longer. Where were the sisters? At last he was able to get directions to the convent. It was early when he arrived, so he sat to rest in an inner courtyard at the invitation of the owner who was just coming home.

When he heard the convent bells summoning the sisters to morning prayer, he rang the monastery bell. The portress opened the door and Fray Juan de la Cruz, exhausted but happy to be in that haven, said, "Daughter, I am Fray Juan de la Cruz. I have just escaped from jail. Please tell the superior that I am here."[7] As soon as she heard this, the prioress, Madre Ana de Los Angeles, rushed to the turnstile. One of the sisters had taken ill and had asked to go to confession, and Madre Ana de Los Angeles, who knew Fray Juan to be an extraordinary confessor, admitted him to the cloister. After hearing the nun's confession, he spoke with the sisters. They were horrified at his condition: worn out, incredibly thin, pale, exhausted, and clothed in his oversized, dirty habit, he presented a pitiful sight. They gave him something to eat and listened to him.

Meanwhile, the friars had discovered Fray Juan's escape and began a search for him. Two friars came to the convent seeking the keys for the church next door, where they thought he might be hiding. When they did not find him in the church, they brought back the keys and tried to discover if the nuns knew of Fray Juan's whereabouts. The portress subtly avoided their questions and the friars left.

Madre Ana de Los Angeles knew Fray Juan de la Cruz could not stay with them long. She contacted a friend of the community, Don Pedro Gonzalez de Mendoza, a cathedral canon and the administrator of the Hospital of Santa Cruz in Toledo. Don Pedro went to the convent and took Fray Juan, disguised in a cassock, to the hospital—a short distance from the very monastery he had just escaped. In fact, he could see the monastery's balcony window.

Fray Juan was free to rest and pray. His great trial was over, but others would follow as he lived his life with God in this community of Discalced Friars.

CHAPTER V

Fray Juan de la Cruz'
Leadership in Andalusia
(1578–1588)

ONCE FRAY JUAN HAD RESTED and recovered somewhat from his ordeal, he was anxious to leave his hiding place in Toledo and rejoin his community. Meanwhile, because of all the problems they were having, the Discalced Friars decided to hold yet another meeting at Almodovar del Campo on October 9, 1578. It lasted only a few days, but the priors and important religious of the Reform gathered there and took a number of decisive steps.[1] Although some opposed the move in light of their terribly delicate position since the arrival of the new Legate a year earlier, the "Chapter" went ahead and elected a "provincial," which was construed as yet another rebellious act. (Once the Legate heard of the election, he excommunicated everyone who had been at the Chapter.) The Chapter members then proceeded to send Fray Nicolás de Jesús María and Fray Pedro de Los Angeles to Rome to explain their position and to seek a separation of the Discalced from the Calced portion of the community. Finally, they named Fray Juan de la Cruz superior of El Calvario, their monastery in Andalusia.

Fray Juan set out for El Calvario accompanied by two servants, pressed on him by Don Pedro Gonzalez de Mendoza, who feared that the long journey alone would be too strenuous for Fray Juan. The trip would have been a difficult one even for someone in excellent health. The weather was still warm and uncomfortable. The dry summer had covered everything in the barren land with a gritty film of sand. Fray Juan passed through the plains and arrived at the more fertile hills and valleys of Andalusia. He had planned to visit the Discalced nuns in Beas. By the time he reached them, he was fatigued and so emaciated that his features were gaunt and drawn. The nuns hardly recognized him. They tried to cheer him up with a song, but even this did not dispel the distance his condition placed between them. He seemed far away.

For the first few days at Beas, Fray Juan was quiet and shy, but as he rested he began gradually to speak more freely with the nuns and to be more relaxed in their company. However, some of the nuns were not impressed with the renowned friar. One day as Fray Juan spoke to the nuns about Madre Teresa, he referred to her as *"hija mia,"* my daughter. This reference annoyed the superior, Madre Ana de Jesús, who really thought the young friar was being rather insolent in speaking of their great foundress as if she were simply an ignorant woman. Though she would later become one of his most fervent disciples, his initial shyness and that one incident kept her from recognizing the great spiritual potential that lay within him. We know this because she wrote to la Madre bemoaning the fact that she and her nuns had no one with whom to speak of spiritual things. In her answer, Madre Teresa praised Fray Juan's qualities so highly that Madre Ana was very surprised. She and her sisters had met a rather common little priest in Fray Juan. Now Madre Ana paid more attention and came to see a deeply spiritual man. With time, the nuns came to know him better and they would learn a great deal from him.

FIGURE 1. *Drawing of Jesus Crucified done by Fray Juan de la Cruz that is kept in the Encarnación Monastery in Avila, Spain.*

FIGURE 2. *A statue of Fray Juan de la Cruz at the Carmelite convent in Lisieux, which St. Thérèse must have seen daily.*

FIGURE 3. *A painting of Fray Juan de la Cruz by St. Thérèse's sister Pauline.*

FIGURE 4. *A painting of Fray Juan de la Cruz that is kept in the Carmel of Ubeda, Spain, where he died.*

Photo: Richard P. Hardy, Ph.D.

FIGURE 5. *In this view of the verdant Segovian countryside, the monastery of Fray Juan can be seen (upper center to the left). To the right stands the church of the Knights Templar of Vera Cruz.*

FIGURE 6. *The Eresma River (Segovia) flows below the Alcazar Palace (above left), and in front of the monastery that Fray Juan de la Cruz had built further up the hill away from the river. It likely inspired some of Fray Juan's poetic imagery.*

FIGURE 7. *Fray Juan de la Cruz depicted in the habit of the Discalced Carmelites.*

Anoymous: 1872

FIGURE 8. *An anonymous ink drawing of Fray Juan de la Cruz, prolific writer on the spiritual life, holding a book and pen.*

FIGURE 9. *The Alcazar Palace in Segovia where Queen Isabella and King Ferdinand were crowned in the late fifteenth century. Fray Juan could see the palace from the caves behind the monastery where he lived from 1588 to 1591.*

Photo: Richard P. Hardy, Ph.D.

FIGURE 10. *The Cathedral of St. Mary in Segovia. The construction of the gothic-style building began in 1525 and was not completed until the seventeenth century. Fray Juan would have seen its progress during his visits to Segovia and his three-year stay there beginning in 1588.*

FIGURE 11. *A painting of Fray Juan de la Cruz at the former Discalced monastery of Pastrana. This is an artistic attempt to portray the vision Fray Juan is said to have had before a painting of the suffering Christ. In this vision Christ asked, "What do you wish from me?" And Fray Juan answered, "To suffer for you."*

FIGURE 12. *A plaque that can be seen on the road leading to the monastery in Segovia that Fray Juan planned and built, as least in part, while living there (1588–1591). The sign reads:* "God is the Spring from which each person draws according to the way one carries the cup."

Courtesy of Sergia Ballini, FSP–ITALY

FIGURE 13. *An anonymous rendering of Fray Juan de la Cruz in Savona, Italy.*

FIGURE 14. *The Church of San Juan de la Cruz, Segovia, where the body of the mystical doctor is kept in the side chapel to the left.*

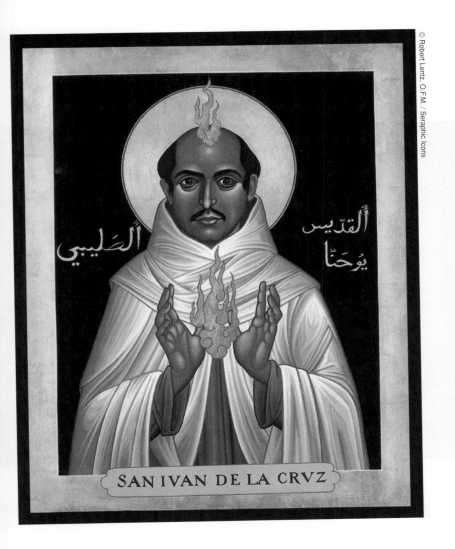

الْقِدِّيس يُوحَنَّا الصَّليبي

SAN IVAN DE LA CRVZ

FIGURE 15. *This beautiful icon, painted by Robert Lentz, has the name of Fray Juan de la Cruz in Arabic to signify his Islamic roots. The flame in Fray Juan's heart and the one coming from his head symbolize the Living Flame of Love filling and transforming his mind and heart.*

FIGURE 16. *The coffin of Fray Juan and the ceiling above it.*

FIGURE 17. *The altar with the coffin containing the remains of Fray Juan de la Cruz in the church of the Discalced Carmelite Friars Monastery in Segovia. This tomb was dedicated in 1927, shortly after Fray Juan de la Cruz was named a Doctor of the Church.*

Icon (detail): Marice Saniola (Capel, Western Australia, Infant Jesus Church, Morely, Western Australia, 1992; Photo: Greg Burke, O.C.D.

FIGURE 18. *This image of Fray Juan captures the gentleness and serenity of the man who so willingly served Christ in others.*

FIGURE 19. *This Roman aqueduct in Segovia would certainly have been a familiar sight to Fray Juan de la Cruz. Built during the Roman occupation (200 BCE–100 CE), the aqueduct, constructed of fitted stones without cement or mortar, still functions today.*

FIGURE 20. *The burial place (early seventeenth century) of Fray Juan de la Cruz in the side chapel of the Discalced Carmelite Friars Church of San Juan de la Cruz in Segovia. His remains rested here until 1927 when they were transferred to the present tomb (see Figure 17).*

FIGURE 21. *A painting of the Spanish mystic in contemplation.*

FIGURE 22. *A statue of the mystical doctor stands behind the altar and coffin of Fray Juan in the side chapel of the Church of San Juan de la Cruz at the Discalced Carmelite Friars Monastery in Segovia.*

FIGURE 23. *A painting of the mystical doctor by an anonymous eighteenth-century artist. The portrait depicts Fray Juan's sense of silence (finger on lips) and mortification (ascetical instrument in right hand). Another version shows the words, "Be silent and work," coming from Fray Juan's mouth.*

FIGURE 24. *One of the best-known religious paintings by Salvadore Dalí inspired by the picture drawn by John of the Cross (see Figure 1).*

El Calvario

After a few days of rest, Fray Juan continued his journey to El Calvario. It was a short distance, but the poor condition of the roads that wended their way through the hills and valleys and his physical weakness made the trip difficult. The thirty Carmelite friars at El Calvario awaited his arrival with apprehension. Some of the friars feared that their new superior would bring rigidity to their monastery. Fray Juan had been among the first to join the Discalced, and his reputation from Medina del Campo and Salamanca had spread through the grapevine of religious gossip. The friars imagined that his imprisonment had made him even harder and more demanding.

When Fray Juan de la Cruz arrived, they were surprised by the gentleness and kindness of the little friar who would take the superior's place while he was in Rome. This newly arrived friar seemed made for the isolated monastery in the Sierra Morenas surrounded by hills and valleys covered with fruit trees, olive groves, and other vegetation. It was an ideal place to pray, rest, and live the life of a Discalced. The contrast to his nine months in a closet cell was bound to rejuvenate Fray Juan.

The friars of El Calvario lived frugally. In fact, their diet consisted mostly of weeds and other vegetation from the fields, which they cooked with a bit of garlic and vinegar. If they had both oil and vinegar, it was a most unusual day. They prayed together in choir as the Rule required and they spent the rest of the time meditating privately in their cells. Fray Juan's cell was as simple as all the other rooms. It was his opinion that everyone should be treated alike, whether a superior or a subject. His bed was no more than a bundle of rosemary and brush woven together for a mattress. A small table and chair were the only other furniture in the room. The friars lived and worked together, and when food was lacking, they still gathered in the refectory where Fray Juan would give the blessing and thank God for having chosen them to suffer a little that day. Life in this monastery was a growing together in God. The friars came to see more clearly how their life together could enhance their life with God, who was present among them in very tangible ways. And they carried this presence with them in their ministries.

Every Saturday Fray Juan would walk to Beas to hear the confessions of the nuns, guide them on their spiritual journey, and celebrate the Eucharist with them. These were days of great joy for the nuns and Fray Juan. One of the nuns, Madre Magdalena del Espiritu Santo, tells of Fray Juan's gentleness and kindness. When he spoke, she realized how much she and her fellow nuns gained from him.[2] They could not meet him and hear his words without seeing how deeply he was united with the God they also served. His physical presence revealed all that he was as God's gift. Experiencing this encouraged the nuns in their community living, prayer, and mortification, which Fray Juan's guidance helped them to see in a new light. In events like this, we find the beginnings of his later commentaries on his poetry. His discussions with the nuns helped Fray Juan to clarify his ideas, and thus they became the stuff from which he created his masterful prose commentaries such as *The Spiritual Canticle* and *The Living Flame of Love*. Through all this, moreover, the sisters learned of his great gentleness, knowledge, and deep humanity.

While at the convent, Fray Juan was never idle. In his free time, he weeded the garden and cultivated flowers. He loved to feel the earth, to be in contact with nature, which so often inspired the poet in him. He was indeed a man rooted in the earth. The wonder of each plant and flower brought him constantly back to the awareness of the Divine throughout creation. Each Monday Fray Juan walked back to El Calvario still bearing the peace and restfulness that his stay at Beas gave him.

Spurred on by the questions and comments of the nuns at Beas, and particularly by their constant urging, Fray Juan de la Cruz began to seriously write commentaries on his poems. He wrote *The Ascent of Mount Carmel* and, at the same time, the first draft of *The Spiritual Canticle*. He also wrote *The Precautions* for the nuns at Beas. This short work consists of a series of admonitions meant to help the religious grow closer to God through their life as committed consecrated Christians. The nuns greatly appreciated this work, and they enjoyed receiving the sketch of Mount Carmel he drew for them.

Despite his success in helping the nuns, he felt sad. He wanted to return to his native Castile. He missed the people, the landscape of fresh mountain pines and the burnt parchedness of the summer in the northern plains. After two years of living in southern Spain, where he felt abandoned and the people were so different from those with whom he had grown up, he was lonely and yearned to see his mother and brother once again. However, his return to Castile would be delayed for several more years. Now he was needed in Baeza.

Baeza

Baeza was an important city in sixteenth-century Spain. With 50,000 inhabitants and a very good university, it was a fine place to begin a new house of religious in Andalusia.

Several leading members of the university in Baeza had heard of the Discalced and were doing everything in their power to have these friars come to establish a monastery in their city. After some discussion, the Discalced Friars decided that Baeza would indeed be an excellent location for a house of studies, and they appointed Fray Juan de la Cruz its founding rector.

Once he had discovered a location to establish a student residence, Fray Juan chose three friars to go with him to establish the new foundation, Colegio de San Basilio, the first Discalced house of studies. The three friars set out on foot for Baeza, leaving El Calvario early on June 13, 1579. They had walked the thirty miles to Baeza by nightfall and prepared the chapel for the next morning's opening Eucharist for the feast of the Holy Trinity.

The colegio was situated not far from the university and very near to the Puerto de Ubeda. Today, the former site of the Colegio de San Basilio is occupied by the Escuela de Artes Aplicados y Oficios Artisticos with its large, modern building and garden, not far from the city's Moorish walls. The colegio, like other Carmelite monasteries, was built on the fringes of the city in a *barrio*. As Fray Juan walked from the colegio to the university, he could see the brown-tiled roof of the cathedral through the arch of the Puerta de Ubeda, its watchtower standing guard. The very narrow cobblestone streets were lined with stone houses crushing in on the tight alleys and blocking a panoramic view. The streets wound their way up and down slight inclines toward the city's center. Once he had arrived at the immense cathedral, with the Fuente de Santa María to the side, he could see the massive stone buildings of the university and church. The ornate stone carvings around and above the doors of the short, square university building remind one of the immortal quality of medieval architecture. It was in this city of intellectuals and *beatas* (laywomen who lived alone in their houses and dressed as religious) that Fray Juan was to spend the next two years.

Fray Juan's life did not change much as the rector of Baeza. Poverty was still a key element of religious life for him. Though the friars lacked mattresses, pillows, and other necessities, Fray Juan was not willing to allow the bursar to go out and get the needed items from benefactors. He would say: "...What is it to be poor if we have everything we need?"[3] As if to prepare his fellow friars for a life of real poverty, he even refused to accept a gift of mattresses and other materials from someone at the university who had witnessed their poverty. To be free from all things so that they could love all things in the Divine: this was his motivation. He also continued to accent the life of recollection, which he maintained should be at the heart of every Discalced Carmelite's life. This recollection allowed each friar and the community as a whole to enflesh the God of love more and more. For days on end, the citizens of Baeza would not see the friars walking the streets. They went out very seldom and even these rare periods outside the monastery were either to go to the university or to visit the sick. Once at a chapter of faults when the friars would confess their infractions before the community and sometimes point out each other's transgressions, the provincial rebuked Fray Juan for not going out more often to visit rich and influential lay people. Fray Juan prostrated himself before the provincial and said that if he used this time instead to ask God to move these people to give what was necessary and they did, would that not be good enough? There was silence. Fray Juan had made his point. His view prevailed. He was always the first to give the right example and, in this way, he set the tone for life in the new colegio.

Fray Juan's days were filled with the ordinary. He cleaned the house, arranged the chapel, and did repairs as needed. He did not use his position as superior to avoid the day-to-day work required in the community. Fray Juan de la Cruz always saw himself as one of the many brothers who lived and worked together. In his spare moments, he would continue his work on *The Ascent of Mount Carmel* and *The Spiritual Canticle*. He prayed and read the Scriptures. Often he slept only two or three hours nightly and spent the remaining hours praying in the chapel. Sometimes the friars would find him lying on the chapel floor with his head on his cape. There he rested with his God.

The liturgy was very important to him. The devotion to common prayer that he always had grew deeper. Not only was he extremely fastidious about the cleanliness of the altar and vestments, but he became creative on special days. For example, at Christmas time he would have plays performed by the friars. With friars dispersed throughout the monastery, acting as the innkeepers of Bethlehem, he and others would take on the role of the holy family. As he stopped at each group of friars, Fray Juan would speak of the wonders of Christmas. His face shone. His features came alive as he spoke of this mystery and his eyes brightened with joy. Doña Maria de Paz, a *beata* of Baeza, spoke of seeing him at different seasons and how his whole body, especially his face, seemed to reveal the mood of the season.[4] Fray Juan was like all human beings whose hearts can be read in their physical appearance if one looks carefully.

He was a man of striking honesty for his time. One day someone came to the colegio with some stipends for Eucharists to be offered on particular dates. Since all the friars already were occupied on those days, Fray Juan ordered that the stipends not be accepted. One of his assistants suggested that one day more or less was not really important, and since they needed the money perhaps they could accept the stipends and offer the Eucharists at a later date. However, Fray Juan firmly maintained that they were to be truthful first and foremost and leave their needs to God. Fray Juan loved authenticity, a key quality of a Christian.

Fray Juan de Santa Eufemia described another striking characteristic of Fray Juan de la Cruz.[5] According to the constitutions of the Order, the superior was to visit the cells of the friars to make sure they were not disobeying any rules. Fray Juan would do this, but, as he went along, he would rattle his rosary, thereby making enough noise to warn the friars that he was coming. He was never out to catch someone doing something wrong. He saw the Rule and its fulfillment as a way of helping others to live out their religious lives more fully.

Fray Juan also showed this human, considerate quality during the community's recreation periods. After supper, the friars would go to a common room to listen to Fray Juan and to relax. His conversations were so fascinating that the friars always left that room rested and laughing. Whether he spoke of ordinary or spiritual things, his hearers were always happy when they departed. In fact, the friars looked forward to their evening encounters so much that those who served the meals often skipped their own afterward in order to be able to hear him and be with him. Only a totally human and compassionate man could inspire such love and devotion.

Fray Juan's compassion came to the fore once again in his concern and care for the sick. The year 1580 was marked by the *catarro universal,* an influenza epidemic that hit all of Spain. Entire families often fell ill at the same time. The family of one of the friars at San Basilio suffered this hardship. So Fray Juan went with this friar to visit his family. They found the family members spread throughout the house in different rooms. Fray Juan spoke with each of them and comforted them as best he could. Back at the colegio, the rooms were filled with his own sick friars and nine others who had been brought there from El Calvario to be treated. Fray Juan changed bed linens and bathed and fed the patients. Sometimes he even cooked for them. In his youth, Fray Juan had learned from his family and his experience in Las Bubas how to tend to the sick. Yet, now the same actions took on a much deeper significance for both him and those who witnessed him in such service. The God whom he loved became the gift he was for everyone. His gentleness and deep concern made him loved even more.

The influenza also struck Medina del Campo and Juan's mother became seriously ill and died shortly afterward. Out of respect for Fray Juan, and because she herself had been so close to the nuns, the Discalced nuns had her buried in their own cemetery. Only his brother Francisco remained, and he would be a great joy to Fray Juan de la Cruz in the closing years of the little friar's life.

While the rector at the colegio, Fray Juan de la Cruz spent a good deal of time in spiritual guidance. Students, some of the *beatas,* and ordinary people sought him out as they made their journey to God. Some of the teachers at the university also came almost daily to reflect with Fray Juan on

Scripture and to receive advice about their own spiritual growth. Among them were Dr. Ojeda, Maestro Sepulveda, Doctors Becerra and Carleval, and Padre Nuñez Marcelo. All were amazed at the exactitude and newness of his interpretation of certain scriptural passages. What they gradually came to realize was that Fray Juan could see Scripture in creative ways because he approached it as the source of his own daily life. It was not simply a question of finding a pertinent text for any given event. Rather, Fray Juan de la Cruz lived each moment of his life so fully that he could then read the Bible and constantly see the newness it offered. He incarnated the Scripture daily because he knew how to plumb its message, leading him to live in an ever more human way and always more concerned about all people.

In Baeza, Fray Juan surprised everyone who knew him with his intense love of nature. He would speak eloquently of the simplest flower in the field. A Spanish sky filled with countless stars would send him into an ongoing praise of the God who had given humanity such beauty. He would often take someone out to the fields and, after having prayed alone, Fray Juan would rejoin him and begin talking about the beauty that surrounded them and the God of whom it spoke.

Yet, despite all the joys that the countryside offered, and all the activity and prayer that kept him more than occupied, Fray Juan de la Cruz was still sad. He openly expresses this in a letter to Madre Catalina de Jesús dated July 6, 1581:

> Although I don't know where you are, I want to write these lines trusting that our Madre will send them on to you if you are not with her. And if it is so—that you are not with her—be consoled with

the thought that you are not as abandoned and alone as I am down here. For after that whale swallowed me up [a biblical allusion to his imprisonment in Toledo] and vomited me out upon this alien port [Andalusia], I have never merited to see her again nor the saints up there. God has done well, for after all, abandonment is a steel file and the endurance of darkness leads to great light.[6]

He ends this letter abruptly, as if totally exhausted by the thoughts of loneliness and darkness he had put down on paper. The night had not finished its work in Toledo. The whole situation must have been almost intolerable, for he sought Madre Teresa's help to get him back north to Castile. Nonetheless, he would have to wait some seven years before he could return to his native region where he always felt more at ease. For now, he continued his work in Baeza. He helped everyone without distinction. He demanded that lay people seeking any assistance from the friars always find an open door. Though he and the other friars were exhausted from people constantly seeking them out, their role was to receive and to help them. Fray Juan knew that as believers in Jesus their lives were to be fully involved in the world in which they lived. His cross was the path to life—to learn to let go is the message of suffering. Baeza was his life *now* and he lived it to the full.

Papal Approval of the Discalced

After much negotiating, the Discalced Carmelites finally achieved what they had sought for so long. On June 22, 1580, Pope Gregory XIII issued a Brief authorizing the separation of the Discalced Carmelites from the Calced. But not until November was Padre Maestro Fray Juan de las Cuevas, a

Dominican, named executor of the Brief. Cuevas called the first legal Chapter of the Discalced, which took place amidst much splendor and pomp on March 3, 1581. The following day Fray Juan de la Cruz was elected one of the definitors who were advisors in the governing of the community, along with Padres Nicolás de Jesús María Doria, Antonio de Jesús, and Gabriel de la Asunción. Though many of the members of the Chapter wanted Fray Juan de la Cruz or Fray Antonio de Jesús as provincial, Padre Jeronimo de la Madre de Dios Gracian was elected. Cuevas favored Gracian and thus swung the vote in his favor.

Fray Juan's election as definitor began a period of intense administrative and spiritual activity that would end only a few months before his death ten years later.

Fray Juan traveled a good deal during his stay at Baeza. He continued to be the confessor and director of the nuns at Beas. However, since he could now go there only once or twice a month, he stayed longer than a day or two as he had when he was in El Calvario. He went to Caravaca for the election of the prioress in June 1581. By November, he was in Avila trying to convince Teresa to personally establish a convent in Granada. Instead, she sent him with some sisters and appointed Madre Ana de Jesús of Beas the superior. From December 8 until January 15, 1582, Fray Juan waited in Beas for the license to establish the convent in Granada. Things moved slowly. When he and the sisters could wait no longer, they set off for Granada and stopped three miles outside the city. The trip had been terribly difficult. Rain had turned the roads into pools of mud and many of them were simply impassable. At Albolete on January 19, 1582, the vicar provincial informed the group of Discalced that the archbishop had still not given his permission for them to set up the convent. Furthermore, they learned that the house they had planned on occupying was suddenly no longer available. Despite all of this, they decided to go ahead. On January 20, the group arrived in Granada at the house of a rich woman, Señora Ana de Peñalosa, who had promised to help them. She would become a great friend and benefactress of Fray Juan de la Cruz in Segovia. Fray Juan then went to the monastery of Los Martires to live with the friars until the sisters had settled in. It would be a much longer and more official stay than he had planned.

Los Martires

The striking natural setting of Los Martires appealed to Fray Juan's personality. To reach the monastery one had to make an exhausting climb up the steep hill on the top of which sits the Alhambra, an ancient Moorish palace. Los Martires lies a little lower than the Alhambra and to its right. Between these monuments to the two great religious traditions of Andalusia lies a small canyon, now filled with trees. The monastery, simple and small, was built in a garden, which originally held conical pits that served as dungeons for the Christians during certain periods of the Moorish occupation of Spain. When the friars took over the property a few years earlier, they planted vines, bushes, and trees. Their pond, supplied with water from the Alhambra, flowed in, as it does today, by means of an aqueduct. From the precipice on which it was built, the monastery overlooked the plains spreading southward far below. A few houses stood at the bottom of the steep incline, but the main part of the city of Granada could not be seen; it lay on the other side of the Alhambra. However, opposite the precipice, with its view of the plains, one could see the foothills and the snow-capped mountains of the Sierra Nevadas to the north. The infinity symbolized by these mountains and the spreading plains below, as well as the beauty of the vegetation and man-made edifices, struck Fray Juan. Here was God's creation in all its variety and wonder.

The friars of Los Martires decided to make use of the prerogative granted to Discalced houses in their new constitutions allowing them to elect as prior anyone in the province, even if he were already a superior in another house. The friars elected Fray Juan de la Cruz as their superior in March 1582. This began his six years of residency in Granada, although the last three years of his term involved so much traveling one can hardly say he actually resided in Granada during that period.

Fray Juan's personality flourished in Granada. A city of incredible beauty, Granada became for him the spring rain that makes the trees and flowers bloom. His ever-present love for the sick, his concern for the poor, and his love of solitude are clearly seen during this period. He might be poor and suffering himself, but that mattered little as long as he could alleviate the pain of others.

One day while he was prior in Granada, one of the brothers became ill. Fray Juan was very concerned and called the doctor. He told Juan that nothing could be done to cure the friar, though there was a costly medicine that would alleviate some of his pain. Without a moment's hesitation, Fray Juan asked for the prescription and had it filled immediately. This is only one example of his genuine care of those who were ill.

Anytime a friar was sick, Fray Juan de la Cruz would visit and stay with him. He would speak with him or spend hours by his bedside in silence, holding his hand, wiping his feverish brow, feeding him. He would talk about something that would help the friar to relax and rest. Sometimes he spoke of God and the love God showered on all human beings, or he would speak about the community, or the weather, or nature's beauty. He adapted his conversation to the needs of the individual. That the sick person be consoled was of greatest importance, but Fray Juan did not find these conversations dull or boring. If he spoke about things that helped another, it was always something that interested him too. He never put on airs. His sincerity was apparent to all observers. One could be sure that whatever Fray Juan said or did, it came from the depths of who he was.

When his duties as vicar provincial obliged Fray Juan to visit several Carmelite houses, he would always ask to see the sick members of the community as soon as he arrived. He seemed to be at home when he stepped into an infirmary, as if he were sixteen again and working in the hospital at Medina del Campo. He would visit with the sick to see how they were. If they had not been eating, he would name different types of food they might want. Once he learned what they would like to eat, he went out and often prepared the food himself, returning to feed the patients as well. Whether the patient was old or young, educated or not, he was their loving brother. Fray Juan's truly remarkable tenderness did not go unnoticed by those who met him.

The famine in Andalusia during 1584 brought his special qualities to the fore. Crops had failed. Food was very scarce. Many people from the country came into the city in search of food and help. Los Martires received many callers looking for food and assistance. Fray Juan and the other friars knew their own supplies were limited, but Fray Juan did not hesitate to give food to all who came. He refused no one. In fact, Fray Juan discreetly sent food to some rather highly placed families who were in need. He did this to spare them from having to lose face by coming to beg at the monastery. Fray Juan constantly showed his love and sensitivity to all kinds of people, whatever their situation.

Fray Juan responded generously, giving freely of his time and efforts. Whether he was at prayer or work, if someone called upon him, he left everything to go to him or her. For him, God was never absent, and so Fray Juan knew whatever he did he was always in the Divine Presence. This deep consciousness of God's presence enabled Fray Juan to bring people to hope even when they wanted to doubt everything. He would show these discouraged people the positive aspects of their lives and thus help them to go on. In dealing with people afflicted by scruples and tempted to despair, he was the perfect example of kindness, patience, openness, understanding, and gentleness. His deep understanding of people enabled him to be a confessor of many people in Granada. Priests, religious, laywomen and laymen, rich and poor came to him because they knew he was a man who understood and, therefore, could be the sacrament of God's presence for them.

In sixteenth-century Spain, the prior of a monastery had a very high social standing. However, Fray Juan was not one to be impressed by such class distinctions or social games. One day while he was helping some workers on the monastery grounds, an important religious superior came to visit him. The porter went out to find Fray Juan, and when the other brothers and workers heard of the eminence of their visitor, they suggested that Fray Juan go in and clean up. But Fray Juan was not about to do anything special. He simply had the porter bring the visitor to him—just as and where he was. On another occasion, a superior from a different religious community came to visit Fray Juan and said: "My dear Father, since you keep yourself here in the monastery and we do not see you in the city, we would think you were the son of some worker." Fray Juan answered him with a touch of annoyance: "Oh, I am not so highly placed a person. I am simply the son of a weaver."[7] His visitor understood.

When Fray Juan spoke, people were impressed because he was so authentic. Fray Martin de San José said: "...Neither before nor since, either in a religious community or outside it, have I heard a person who could treat of God so beautifully."[8] Fray Juan's words were his own, nurtured by his prayer and by interaction with his fellow human beings. While his studies surely provided him with a great deal of knowledge, the warmth of his words came from an intimate experience of the God of whom he spoke. Listening to him, one always became calm and serene. It seemed as if all difficulties disappeared. People were ready to go on living with enthusiasm. Whether it was a homily he gave, a short talk, or simply a conversation, the effect on his listeners was the same: they were filled with peace and love. Fray Juan Evangelista, who had been a novice under Fray Juan and was his companion for the last years of his life, said that when Fray Juan would speak to the friars during recreation, he would most often speak of God, but never in an overly serious way. He would speak of him in such a way that the brothers would laugh and go out filled with great joy.[9] Fray Juan, like the psalmists of biblical times, was an intimate friend of God. God was so real, so close, that he could be part of one's sense of humor.

Fray Juan de la Cruz was certainly not a staid, serious, unapproachable man. Yet, he still loved solitude, which provided him with a sense of freedom. His mind and heart could wander with God over all the things of beauty and life. When alone he would read the Scriptures and let God's word sink deeply into his heart. Solitude was not just a chance to get away; it made it possible for him to love God and his brothers more fully. Solitude meant being with God and, in this way, to become more God-like. To reach this point of true solitude, the world and people in particular became very special to him. He urged his brothers to solitude. He and they had chosen a life of recollection and withdrawal from the fantasies of society. He knew he had not withdrawn from the world, only from the games of people who set up classes and divisions. Solitude with his God brought Fray Juan to see more clearly the beauty of the world and the equality of human beings. His father and mother had suffered because of society's rules. Many considered his brother Francisco a humiliating creature because of his poverty. Solitude taught Fray Juan the truth about the world, and, with this insight, he could become more deeply human and simple.

In Granada, as in the other monasteries, his cell was the poorest. It was small and narrow, furnished with only a small table and bench, a bed with straw for a mattress, and a small painted crucifix on the wall. Only a Bible and a *Flos Sanctorum* adorned the table. He wore an old habit. Whenever he needed something, he would go to the storeroom and choose the oldest and most worn item, saying that it was good enough for him.

His days in Granada were full. He would visit the nuns at the monastery just below Los Martires. He would sit on one side of the grate in the speaking parlor while the nuns would gather on the other to listen to him speak for about an hour. He constantly told them to let go of all that was not God. He guided them, listened, explained, and helped them all to grow in God. He did this as well with the nuns at Beas, whom he continued to visit regularly.

On one of his trips to Beas, a woman holding a small baby approached Fray Juan and said that the child was his and he should provide for its keep. Fray Juan asked the woman about the mother and was told she was a fine woman who had never been outside the city of Granada. Then he asked the woman the child's age. On learning that the child was a year old, Fray Juan said: "Let us praise God for this miracle, because I've been in Granada for less than a year and I've never been here before."[10] He chuckled all the way to Beas and, when he arrived, he could hardly wait to tell the superior about the incident. And he laughed as he told her the story.

Further Travels and Writings

On May 1, 1583, Fray Juan was in Almodovar del Campo for the second Chapter of the Reform. The provincial, Padre Gracian, urged a more active role for the community. Fray Juan de la Cruz opposed this and argued that the Discalced were primarily a group of contemplatives and that any activity that took them away from this should be avoided. However, he did say that some apostolic work was part of their lives as religious. He simply wished to avoid reducing the contemplative dimension to second place.

After his trip to Almodovar, when he was not visiting Beas or teaching the nuns at Granada, Fray Juan would write. In the year of the famine, 1584, Fray Juan wrote the first draft of *The Spiritual Canticle*, the poem *The Living Flame of Love*, and perhaps even the commentary.[11] Madre Ana de Jesús heard Fray Juan talk about his poem *The Spiritual Canticle* and urged him to write down his commentaries. After some persistence, she finally succeeded in getting him to write down his reflections in an orderly fashion. The process was rather simple. After speaking with the nuns, he would return to his monastery and think about some of the themes of which they had spoken. Then he would write these thoughts down. In this way, he was able to complete *The Spiritual Canticle* (and at the same time *The Ascent of Mount Carmel* and *The Dark Night*) and then, in about fourteen days, the commentary of *The Living Flame of Love*. He wrote the commentary on *The Living Flame of Love* at the insistence of Ana de Peñalosa. The period at Granada was the most literarily productive of his life. His major works were complete, and only some revisions of the second writing of *The Spiritual Canticle* and *The Living Flame of Love* were yet to be done toward the end of his life.

In 1585, a new period of administration and travel began. In February, Fray Juan traveled the eighty-four miles between Granada and Malaga to establish the convent of Discalced nuns in this seashore city. The mountains that formed a backdrop to the city thoroughly enticed Fray Juan. His love for this convent was due at least in part to its idyllic setting. By May 10, Fray Juan was in Lisbon for the General Chapter.

While in Lisbon, he was invited several times to go to see a Madre María de la Visitación, the prioress of the Dominican convent of the Anunciada. She was well known in Portugal and Spain for the raptures and ecstasies she purportedly experienced as well as the stigmata. She had impressed the prominent people—theologians and priests among them—who met her. When Fray Juan returned to Granada after being elected second definitor and vicar provincial, he was asked if he had met Madre María de la Visitación. He responded, "I did not see the nun, nor did I desire to do so, because I would not think much of my own faith if I thought it would grow one iota by seeing her."[12] Fray Juan did not build his faith on ecstasies and visions, but purely upon trust in God. As it turned out, the nun was later shown to be a fraud.

As vicar provincial, Fray Juan was obliged to travel throughout the region of Andalusia a good deal. As he traveled, he would sing psalms and hymns, read Scripture passages, and pray. He found that the beautiful rugged landscape of southern Spain lent itself to constant prayer. Whenever he had to spend a night over during a trip, he would sleep on a blanket on the floor. He normally had little sleep and used the time he saved to pray and reflect. His new position would provide him with ample material for this reflection.

Between 1585 and June of 1588, Fray Juan seemed to be on the road continually. In the fall of 1585, he attended the adjournment of the Chapter in Pastrana. On his way back to Granada, he presided over the reelection of Ana de Jesús as prioress in January 1586. In 1586, he founded a priory at Cordoba, visited Sevilla, Ecija, and Cordoba, and fell ill at Guadalcazar. At Cordoba, the stone wall on which laborers were working fell onto the section of the monastery where Fray Juan was in his cell. The friars and laborers frantically removed the rubble, fearing that Fray Juan may have been crushed to death. However, when they found him, Fray Juan was crouched in a corner. He laughingly said that the Virgin Mary had protected him with her cape, indicating a stone statue of the Virgin that stood above him in the corner he had rushed to for protection when he heard the wall falling.

When he fell ill at Guadalcazar, not far from Cordoba, part of Fray Juan's ascetical practices were revealed. A friar came to apply some oil to relieve a pain in Fray Juan's side caused by an abscessed lung. He discovered a chain around Fray Juan's waist that he had worn so long it was partly embedded in his flesh. With Fray Juan's consent, the friar removed it. Nothing more is known about such practices after this.

Once he had recovered sufficiently, Fray Juan continued his journeys. The rest of 1586 found him in Madrid, La Manchuela, Granada, Caravaca, Beas, Bujalance, and again in Madrid in December. Another year of travel was his lot in 1587, but in June of 1588, at the first Chapter General of the Discalced at Madrid, Fray Juan was appointed first definitor and counselor general, and on August 10, he assumed the position of prior in Segovia. He was back in his Castile, but his stay would be short and fraught with problems.

CHAPTER VI

The Final Years: Segovia and Ubeda
(1588–1591)

AFTER YEARS OF WAITING AND HOPING, Fray Juan de la Cruz had resigned himself to his Andalusian exile and began his final three years in glory. When he attended the General Chapter in Madrid on June 19, 1588, he was elected first definitor. This meant that he was in charge of the Consulta, the advisory Council of the Order, whenever Padre Doria, the vicar general, was absent. (In fact, this meant that Fray Juan presided over the Consulta for almost the whole first year.) Doria was very happy with this arrangement since he and Fray Juan had been of the same mind, and he felt he could continue to count on his support. Doria could not countenance opposition to his own ideas, yet he should have known that eventually Fray Juan might take a position different from his own. Initially, however, Fray Juan found himself in a rather pleasant situation.

Besides his position on the Consulta, Fray Juan was also appointed prior of Segovia. Ironically, the monastery there had been founded on May 3, 1586, through the instigation of Fray Juan when he was still in Granada. Doña Ana de Mercado y Peñalosa, who had helped the Discalced nuns when they first arrived in Granada, was fulfilling her husband's will that either a hospital or a monastery be built in his native city of Segovia. Fray Juan encouraged her to build a monastery for the

Discalced. By the time Fray Juan arrived as its prior, the Discalced had already been living in the former Trinitarian monastery for two years.

Renovated and restored, the monastery still stands just outside the city across the Eresma River. Facing the monastery, and towering above it on the cliffs that drop sharply to the river, stands the royal palace, the Alcazar, rising like a Spanish galleon from the valley below. Behind the monastery are small gardens reaching up to a natural wall. Within the rocky surroundings are caves from which one can see the beautiful panorama of this old Roman city.

Originally, the monastery was very close to the river. Hence, the building was very damp. Later, the friars decided to build living quarters further up the hill away from the gurgling water. When Fray Juan arrived in August 1588, he saw to the beginning of the new monastic construction. He did not just oversee the work, but he also designed a special aqueduct system and then worked with the laborers on its construction. Much of the work was done in the winter, but the snow and cold did not stop Fray Juan. Barefooted and having only his worn habit for protection against the cold winds, he gathered stones and carried them to where the masons would place them. Despite the weather, he enjoyed the manual work, which suited him, being with the men, and seeing the monastery develop. In addition, he was able to pray while he worked. He was more and more able to find God among these fellow workers as well as in his fellow friars.

In his prayer, work, and conversations, the world of God and the world of human beings became one for Fray Juan. He truly did live with God. Everything became a symbol of

God's presence and the very thought of God made creatures and creation more present to him as well. He wrote: "And here lies the remarkable delight of this awakening: the soul knows creatures through God and not God through creatures."[1] Union with God brought him to love and to see more fully the world in which he lived. It rooted him in this life, in this creation of his God.

Fray Juan's life was extremely active in the Segovian period. In the absence of the vicar general that first year, Fray Juan had to handle a multitude of administrative details connected with his role as superior of the Order. The construction continued, and he gave spiritual advice to some of the nuns in Beas and Granada by correspondence. In the meantime, Doña Ana de Mercado y Peñalosa had moved to Segovia. She and her niece sought the spiritual direction of Fray Juan at the monastery itself, and he frequently visited them at their home as well. While in the home of Doña Ana de Mercado y Peñalosa, he would speak with her servants about their daily routine as well as of God and their path to the Compassionate One. Many people went to the monastery to seek out Fray Juan. Don Juan de Orozco y Covarrubias, archdeacon of Cuéllar and canon of Segovia, and Diego Muñoz de Godoy, canon of Segovia, both knew Fray Juan. Their visits with him always left them impressed. However, Dr. Villegas, the canon penitentiary, is the man whom most witnesses remarked on in a special way.

In addition to his duties as penitentiary, Dr. Villegas was also the confessor of the Discalced nuns in Segovia. No doubt, he had been asked to perform this ministry because of his deep and stable spiritual life. Fray Juan's close involvement with the nuns and his administration of the community meant that his advice on such an appointment was always closely heeded. It is no wonder that Dr. Villegas visited Fray Juan often. The two men would walk together into the garden behind the monastery and then sit on the ground together and talk for four or five hours at a time. They would speak about their lives and God's presence with them. Their friendship grew stronger as time went on, and Fray Juan thoroughly enjoyed the serene hours he spent with Dr. Villegas. He liked only one other person's company as much: that of his brother.

Fray Juan's beloved brother Francisco also came to visit him. Now that Juan was in Castile once more, it was easier for them to see each other. Francisco would come expecting to stay a day or two, but Fray Juan would urge him to stay on for another day, and yet another, until finally Francisco would simply have to leave to get back to his family. Sometimes weeks elapsed before he returned home. Though Fray Juan was a superior, and hence had great social standing, he was not about to hide his poor brother from others. He would introduce Francisco to high and low alike as his "...brother, who is my greatest treasure on earth." Fray Juan never attempted to change his brother or make him more presentable socially. He felt that neither poverty nor ignorance makes any person less a human being than another.

During one of these visits, Fray Juan told Francisco of a unique experience. It seems that one day as Fray Juan was in prayer before a picture of Christ carrying the cross,[2] he heard an interior voice calling his name. This happened several times. Finally, he said inwardly: "Here I am." And the voice said: "What reward would you like to have from me for all you have done and all you have suffered?" Fray Juan de la Cruz responded: "To suffer and to be looked down upon." After having told Francisco this story, Fray Juan added: "So, if you see me with trials, don't worry, Francisco, for these are what I have asked for from the Lord. He will help me to live them out and so to grow more deeply." Those trials would indeed come, but not immediately.

Despite his many activities, Fray Juan cultivated his sense of poverty and solitude so that he could effectively minister to others. According to his usual practice, when Fray Juan arrived in Segovia he chose the most obscure cell. Again, it was a very small room found under a staircase adjoining the choir section of the chapel. His bed was a few boards, and another board attached to the wall became his writing table. His cell was as plain and simple as his food. He ate little and fasted according to the Rule. When something special was sent into the monastery, he would give it to the monks while he ate the normal fare. His times of prayer became more frequent. His special moments of prayer were most often at night while the others slept. Like many other creative people, Fray Juan did not need much sleep; two or three hours a night sufficed, and the rest of the time, he could be found in the chapel kneeling with his arms outstretched or looking out a monastery window at the clear, star-filled Segovian sky, enthralled by the beauty God had showered on the world. When he had some spare time, he would go up to one of the small caves in the cliffs behind the monastery, and there he would pray in quiet as he watched the birds flying in and out of the crevices of the rocks. These times strengthened him. They were very normal parts of the daily rhythm that flowed naturally in his life. The busy yet calm and prayerful moments were important preparations for what was to come.

In 1590, at an Extraordinary Chapter, Fray Juan disagreed with some ideas Padre Doria put before the assembly. The most contentious issue concerned the Discalced nuns. While Doria wanted them to be governed by the Consulta (a procedure that would have complicated their affairs), the nuns wanted to be governed by a person appointed by the Consulta. Fray Juan took their side and this annoyed Doria so much that he began to plan how he could be rid of him.

His opportunity came at the General Chapter held on June 1, 1591. Fray Juan once more opposed Doria's excess in legislating policy for the community. Fray Juan again took up the position of the nuns and defended Padre Gracian, whom he felt was being treated unfairly. Though some of the Chapter members agreed with him privately, publicly they sided with the Vicar General. Fray Juan was not elected to the Consulta and was removed from his post as prior of Segovia. During the Chapter, Fray Juan offered himself as one of the twelve Discalced who were needed to help their province in Mexico. The offer was accepted, but that decision was later reversed. After many years in important administrative positions, the little man was once again an ordinary friar. He did not mind this very much, although he was concerned about the direction the Order was taking.

Fray Juan was about to begin a new ministry, and he went first to La Peñuela to await his departure for the New World. He was not feeling well when he set out, and the long trip exhausted him. Nonetheless, he began to rework some of his writings at this time. The solitude and quiet of this Andalusian retreat was conducive to this work, and he produced the second edition of *The Spiritual Canticle* and *The Living Flame of Love* during this period. This activity was in addition to the normal duties in the monastery. A letter he wrote to Doña Ana de Mercado y Peñalosa on August 19, 1591, provides some insight into how Fray Juan felt.

> I mentioned in the other letter how I desire to remain in this desert of La Peñuela, where I arrived about nine days ago and which is about six leagues north of Baeza. I like it very much, glory to God, and I am well. The vastness of the desert is a great help to the soul and body, although the soul fares very poorly. The Lord must be desiring that it have its spiritual desert. Well and good if it be for his service; His Majesty already knows what we are of ourselves. I don't know how long this will last, for Padre Fray Antonio de Jesús threatens from Baeza that he will not leave me here for long. Be that as it may, for in the meanwhile I am well off without knowing anything, and the life of the desert is admirable. This morning we have already returned from gathering our chickpeas, and so the mornings go by. On another day we shall thresh them. It is nice to handle these mute creatures, better than being badly handled by living ones. God grant that I may stay here. Pray for this, my daughter. But even though I am so happy here, I would not fail to come should you desire. Take care of your soul.... Look after your health and do not fail to pray when you can.[3]

La Peñuela suited him. He was now far from the bickering and the political maneuvering of the Consulta and various factions in the Order. There is no doubt that his rejection at the General Chapter hurt him, but he relished this time of quiet and solitude to recover from the pain (and perhaps even bitterness) that his letter reveals.

He was soon to discover, however, that something was going on behind his back. One of the definitors, Padre Diego Evangelista, elected in the Madrid Chapter, was given the task of going to two or three monasteries in Andalusia to investigate the former provincial, Padre Gracian. To accomplish this assignment thoroughly, he was given the title of Visitor General with rather sweeping powers and authority. However, he did not confine himself to the case of Padre Gracian. He also attempted to discredit Fray Juan. He asked questions in an awkward fashion and scandalized some of the nuns by the suggestions implicit in his questions. He attempted to impute evil actions to Fray Juan, and when the sisters did not answer the way he wanted, he would interpret their responses. He was not beyond changing the content of what they had said. There were members of the community who hated Fray Juan, and they believed the stories Padre Diego was perpetrating. Others were indifferent. Those who were devoted to him were horrified and told Fray Juan, who was deeply hurt. Not even the seclusion of La Peñuela could harbor him from the pain of an unjust attack. Yet Fray Juan refused to allow anyone to speak harshly about the man who was maligning him. He maintained this attitude even during his intense illness. Without encountering any strong opposition to his methods, Padre Diego Evangelista continued his attempts to have Fray Juan thrown out of the Order. Later, when he heard of Fray Juan's death, Padre Diego expressed regret that he had died before he could be expelled.

By the beginning of September 1591, Fray Juan's physical condition worsened. His right leg was inflamed and very painful, and he developed a fever. Finally, it was clear he had to get medical help. On September 21, 1591, he wrote again to Doña Ana de Mercado y Peñalosa:

> I received here in La Peñuela the packet of letters the servant brought me. I greatly appreciate your concern. Tomorrow I am going to Ubeda for the cure of a slight bout of fever. Since it has been returning each day now for more than a week and does not leave me, it seems I shall need the help of medicine. Yet I plan to return here immediately, for I am indeed very happy in this holy solitude.[4]

Fray Juan's superiors gave him the choice of going to Ubeda or Baeza for medical treatment. Many encouraged him to go to Baeza where he was well known and better medical facilities were available. However, Fray Juan simply wanted to rest. Knowing he would have all kinds of visitors in Baeza, he chose to go to Ubeda, despite the fact that he knew it was a relatively new monastery with few resources, and that the prior, Padre Francisco Crisostomo, did not like him. Padre Francisco Crisostomo had been a member of the community of which Fray Juan was the superior. Fray Juan had had to reprimand him, and Padre Francisco never forgot this. Now he was about to have his revenge.

The trip was not extremely long, but Fray Juan's physical condition made it seem like ages. The paths were rough. The roads were dusty. The autumn sun beat down on the sick friar and his companion. Fray Juan had not been able to eat for some time. His leg pained him more than ever; he felt feverish and nauseated most of the time. When he caught sight of the narrow, winding streets of Ubeda, Fray Juan was delighted. The yellowish-brown buildings that lined the rough stone streets brought Fray Juan a sense of relief. He knew he would soon rest in a monastery cell. Upon his arrival at the monastery, the monks greeted him very warmly, especially Fray Alonso de la Madre de Dios, who had been one of his novices in Granada. However, the prior was not so welcoming. His monastery was already having financial difficulties and he saw Fray Juan's arrival as just another problem. He made that clear to the sick friar who had come for a cure.

The entrance of the room, which was to be the final living quarters of Fray Juan on this earth, was a very low doorway. Fray Juan did not have to lower his head because he was so short, but an average-sized person would have to bend down to peer into the tiny cell. The room barely had space for its single piece of furniture, a rough wooden bed. The ceiling was so low it gave one the impression of being in a poorly constructed box. As fall faded into winter, the cold winds blew right through the room; cracks and drafts were everywhere. But Fray Juan was grateful for a place to rest.

The day after his arrival, Fray Juan de la Cruz attended all the community functions. Though still ill and tired, he went to prayer, meals, and recreation with the other friars. The prior had ordered him to do so. He was not to receive any special treatment. When his illness forced him to remain in bed rather than go to the refectory, the prior summoned him to rebuke him for his disobedience. A few days later, however, his sickness became worse and it became clear that he had *erysipelas*, a disease of the nerve endings, which today can be cured with antibiotics. What had begun as a very small boil now broke out into a series of very painful sores. A doctor was called.

When Dr. Ambrosia de Villarreal arrived at the tiny cell and saw the patient, he knew what he had to do. It was necessary to scrape and cut the infected areas and remove the diseased flesh. No anesthetic was available. When he cut and removed the flesh the pain was incredible. Yet, Fray Juan did not utter a sound. As the days went on, his condition grew worse. His flesh was literally rotting and pus flowed constantly from his wounds. Many bandages were used daily. The surgical cutting continued as well, but the patient did not improve.

Soon the news spread that a saint was dying in the Discalced monastery. Many people came to visit him from outside the monastery. Several people sent him special gifts or offered him their services. The friars of the monastery itself went to see him often. All of this annoyed the prior more and more. Finally, he refused to allow any of the friars to visit Fray Juan without his express permission. The prior himself went to see Fray Juan and did all he could to make him uncomfortable. During his visits he would tell Fray Juan how imperfect he was and how much bad example he gave to the other religious of the house. The prior saw him as far too relaxed and careless in his religious observance and told him so. He accused Fray Juan of seeking out too much comfort and even of rejoicing in his illness and in the attention he received. The prior refused to obtain the proper food and medicine Fray Juan required. Then the prior ordered the infirmarian, Fray Bernardo de la Virgen, who slept in Fray Juan's room to care for him at night, to cease being Fray Juan's nurse. This was too much for Fray Bernardo. He wrote to the provincial, Fray Antonio de Jesús, to tell him what was happening. When the news of this cruel treatment reached him, Fray Antonio immediately went to Ubeda.

In the last days of November 1591, Fray Antonio arrived at the monastery in Ubeda. He reprimanded the prior severely and ordered that Fray Juan be given everything he needed, and if necessary he would pay for it all himself. Furthermore, he wanted to spend some time with his former companion of Duruelo. With other friars present, he began speaking about what they had suffered during the early days of the Reform. Fray Juan became visibly impatient and reminded Fray Antonio that they had promised not to speak of such things. Though the provincial was silent for a while, the persistence of the friars who wanted to know all about it won the day. Little by little, Fray Antonio revealed a great deal about those early days—much to Fray Juan's dismay.

The little friar's disease was spreading rapidly. He now had terribly deep and excruciatingly painful ulcers and tumors on his legs and back. He was wasting away; not much flesh remained on his tiny frame. One day the friars tried to move him, but he insisted on moving himself, and they discovered the reason as he dragged himself along: a large tumor on his back had caused him severe pain as they tried to lift him. They hung a rope from the ceiling over his head so that Fray Juan could grab it and pull himself up to change positions from time to time. Just before his death, as he was pulling himself up, he said: "Thank God I am light."[5] He had not lost his sense of humor despite his pain.

And his pain was more than physical. He had already heard of Fray Diego's attempts to have him thrown out of the Order. A pouch of letters he had received telling him of what was happening hung at the head of his bed. Shortly before he died, Fray Juan ordered that this pouch and the letters it contained be burned before him. He wanted to leave nothing behind to cause anyone problems after his death. Even as he was dying, he would not allow anyone to say anything about Fray Diego despite the dishonest things he was doing.

In all of this, people tried to alleviate his pain and distract him from his thoughts. One of the brothers suggested he get some musicians to come and play for Fray Juan. Interestingly enough, at first Fray Juan agreed providing it was not too much trouble. The musicians arrived and began playing outside his window. Then Fray Juan reconsidered. He called the friar back and asked him to pay the musicians and send them away with thanks. He was concerned that perhaps the music would distract him from a fuller attention to the "inner music" he was hearing. He knew he could still grow if he lived out every moment of the life he was given here and now; sometimes he could do nothing else. One day when the provincial was speaking to him, Fray Juan said: "My dear Father, please excuse me if I cannot be attentive to what you are saying because my whole being is racked with pain." He could hardly pray. He could only live his final days hoping that he would not fail to be faithful. When the provincial told him that he would soon receive the reward he had suffered for so much, Fray Juan responded: "Do not tell me that, Father. Don't, please. Tell me my sins." Then he remained silent and closed his eyes.

A week before Fray Juan's death, Dr. Villarreal realized that he was nearing the end and decided it was time to inform him. Hesitantly, one of the brothers said to Fray Juan: "The doctor has told us that the end is near." Upon realizing that he was dying, Fray Juan's face lit up. Finally, after all this pain, it would soon be over. Yet, he lingered on for another week.

On Friday, December 13, 1591, Fray Juan knew instinctively that his death was close at hand. He asked to see the prior and begged forgiveness for all the difficulties he had caused him and the friars. The prior made excuses for not being able to offer him more because of the poverty of the house. The day was silent and cold. Occasionally, Fray Juan would ask what time it was; he seemed obsessed with it. He would then close his eyes. Now and then, the brothers thought he had died, but he was only resting quietly. When Fray Juan opened his eyes, he looked at the crucifix at his bedside, kissed it, and returned to his silence. Around five in the afternoon, he again asked the time and requested the Sacrament of the Sick (Extreme Unction as it was then known). He recited the prayers along with the other friars. Then he asked their forgiveness for the bad example he had given them.

When the provincial insisted he speak some words to them all, Fray Juan de la Cruz urged them to always obey the Rule and the superior, to love each other, and to live in harmony. Then, with profound tenderness, he made the sign of the cross over them all. The rest of the evening, he wanted to be alone. With just a few people around him, he prayed and kissed the crucifix. His pain was intense. At 11:30 P.M. he asked the time once more. Then he said: "The time is near, please call my brothers." Fourteen brothers, as many as could fit, crowded into the tiny room with lighted candles. The other brothers remained in the hall just outside the door. The smell of burning wax filled the little space. The lights flickered, casting shadows on the walls as the friars recited the *De Profundis*. Just before midnight, the dying man again asked the time. Then some of the other monks nervously looked for the prayers of departure. When Fray Juan heard the rustling of pages, he looked at them and said: "Leave it, for the love of God. Be quiet." A few minutes later, the prior began saying the prayers for the dying and Fray Juan asked him to read instead some passages from the Song of Songs. As these were read Fray Juan kept repeating: "What marvelous pearls! What marvelous pearls!..."

The bell rang for matins. Fray Juan asked, "What was that?" "The bell calling the brothers to matins," they answered. "Glory to God! I shall say them in heaven," he said, looking at each one as if giving them a personal message. Once more he kissed the cross, closed his eyes, and said, *Into your hands I commend my spirit.*[6]

Only moments after midnight, on December 14, 1591, Fray Juan de la Cruz, the orderly of Las Bubas, the first friar of the Reform, the prisoner of Toledo, the first definitor, the lover of Jesus, the one who lived with God, passed into eternity. His death was as his life: gentle, tender, compassionate, and loving.

The night was finished. The "Nada" for whom he had searched now embraced him fully. He remained the one rooted in creation, the creation of his God whom he loved so ardently.

EPILOGUE

ONE WOULD THINK THAT THE DEATH of this friar would have ended the drama and mystery that marked his life, but this was not the case. As soon as Fray Juan was dead, the friars gently cleansed his emaciated body, clothed it in his old habit, and prepared for those who would come from Ubeda and the surrounding areas to pay their final respects to the man they had loved. The slight smile on his face—the same smile that had gently encouraged so many people in their trials and proved an enigma to others who were less open to see the transcendent God who broke into this world in and through the life of Fray Juan de la Cruz—suggested the peace in which he had died.

During the months of his illness, when he was confined to his bed in the monastery of Ubeda, people began collecting various objects that had touched him. The bandages which wrapped his wounds were especially important to those who wanted to keep a memento of the man. People are instinctively drawn to keep things that are connected with those whose lives have somehow captured the greatness to which human beings aspire. Though he was not a national hero, something about him had captivated the minds and hearts of many people, especially the "non-persons": the poor. He had been one of them and they knew it. The woman who had spent days washing and preparing his bandages during his last weeks knew it. The friar who had slept in his room during his illness knew it.

The friars who were just beginning their religious lives at Ubeda at the time of his illness knew it. So, each in their own way tried to preserve what they could of his presence, a presence which they knew could be rendered concrete by pieces of bandages, of his habit, and even of his flesh. Such things became sacraments of his enduring presence. His fellow friars began taking pieces of his habit and other objects that he had touched as they laid his body on the heavy wooden table that would henceforth have a new value because his body had rested on it.

Word had spread during his illness that this monastery housed a special friar. The doctor could not hide his surprise at the strength and patience of his charge. He would tell people about this little man's incredible approach to life, to suffering, and even to death itself. "How could he be so utterly gentle and human in the face of such suffering and anguish?" The laundry woman had also heard of the man whose bandages she washed and she, too, spread the stories she heard about him. The menial task of washing his bandages gradually became more meaningful to her. It was a chance for her to soothe suffering and she put more and more of her heart into it. Along with the stories of his final days came occasional details of his life. His own religious community had imprisoned and tortured him. He had deeply loved his mother and brother despite what most people thought about the necessity of "detachment" from such love. He had spent his life loving people who were in difficulty; he especially loved the poor and the uneducated. In short, even for those who had never met him personally, his life gave a unique sense that God, who had shown himself in Jesus, was indeed a lover of humanity, especially of those whom society regards as unimportant.

There were not many people in that town of Ubeda who had not heard of him on that chilly December 14.

Consequently, when the monastery bells rang around one in the morning, groups of people began to move through the streets toward the monastery. In the chilling winter rain, with the wind blowing and whistling through the streets, the town on the hillside began to come alive. Men and women walked toward the tolling sounds that beckoned them to see for themselves the man they had heard about so often in the past weeks. The poor, who constituted the majority of the inhabitants of Ubeda, walked shoulder to shoulder with the rich. They entered the monastery hall to see the friar's withered body laid on the table surrounded by thick wax candles. The smell of the burning wax filled the room as they kissed his feet and hands. While the friars of the Discalced watched and tried to prevent them from doing so, people tore off little pieces of his habit to take home with them.

By the following morning, those who had not heard the bell, or had not understood its meaning, learned what had happened and joined the crowd at the monastery. The crowd became so dense that the religious of the monastery had difficulty clearing a path so that they could take the body of Fray Juan de la Cruz to the chapel. The scene of the night before was repeated: people came in to kneel before the body and to kiss Juan's feet and hands, and they tried to get a memento to take home to remind them of the little friar's presence. A Dominican friar who had known Fray Juan actually planned to cut off one of the fingers from the frail body, but was hindered from doing so. However, the crowd was so great that some people actually succeeded in obtaining not only parts of his habit, but also small pieces of his body.

Gradually order was established and the service for the dead commenced. During the whole of the Eucharist, both the lay people and clergy realized that this was not simply the funeral service of an ordinary friar. Rather, they recognized it as the celebration of a man who had shown how deeply God's love could be incarnated in a human being and how warmly that love could go out compassionately toward others. There were certainly some present who did not like the man, but they, too, saw that the general feeling was one of admiration. Dr. Becerra, Fray Juan's friend from his days in Baeza, preached the homily. He noted that this was not so much an occasion to seek God's mercy as an opportunity to render thanks for the gift that each of them had received through the life of Fray Juan de la Cruz. Here indeed was a saint, even if people did not realize the full implications of that in Fray Juan. When the Eucharist was over and the prayers for the dead said according to the ancient ritual, the people carried the body to its grave, but the burial was not to be the end of the unfolding drama.

Señora Ana de Peñalosa, Fray Juan's close friend who had enabled him to establish the monastery of the Discalced in the city of Segovia several years earlier, believed that his body should rest in that city rather than in Ubeda. So she asked Fray Nicolás de Jesús María, Vicar of the Discalced, to grant permission for the body to be taken from Ubeda to Segovia. Fray Nicolás acceded to her request and drew up letters that ordered the prior of Ubeda to give the body to those who presented him with these papers. In 1592, some nine months after Fray Juan's death, Joan de Medina Baballos went to

Ubeda and presented the letters to the prior. That evening, Baballos and two other men, the prior, and two religious, disinterred the body. They discovered that it was still intact, though certainly dried out. They had expected the body to be completely decomposed. So, rather than take the whole body, they cut off one finger to take back to Señora Ana de Peñalosa and returned the corpse to its grave, planning to remove it when it had decomposed.

Finally, in 1593, assuming that the body had decomposed sufficiently to allow it to be transported, the benefactress and friend of Fray Juan once again sent Joan de Medina Baballos to Ubeda to gather the remains. When Joan arrived in Ubeda, the same scene from the year before was repeated. Baballos presented the letters to the superior. Around eleven that night, the laymen and religious went quietly to the grave to remove Fray Juan's body. But once again, they found it incorrupt. This time, however, they decided to take the body anyway. By midnight, the small cortege unobtrusively left Ubeda for the north. The secrecy was important because they feared that if the townspeople discovered what was happening, a great scene of protest would erupt. To maintain secrecy on their journey to Madrid, they placed the body in an inconspicuous box and traveled through Baeza and other cities under cover of night.

Before entering Madrid, Baballos sent word to Señora Ana de Peñalosa and her brother that they would soon be entering the city with the body. Preparations were made at the convent of the Discalced. When the cortege approached the convent, the doors were opened and, in the presence of some of his closest friends and associates, Fray Juan's body reentered the monastery he had visited several years earlier. They removed an arm for relics and put a new habit on Fray Juan's body. Then the cortege continued on its way to Segovia where they would bury Fray Juan in the monastery where he had felt so much at home.

Segovia received the body with the same tumultuousness that had characterized the wake and funeral in Ubeda some two years earlier. After the arrival at the monastery, word spread quickly through the city that Fray Juan had finally returned. Large crowds came down the hill from the city center to view the body. People paid their respects to this man whom few had actually seen while he lived, but about whom all had heard. They gave rosaries and other religious objects to the friars who guarded the body so that they might touch them to the body before returning them to their owners who then honored them as relics.

When the citizens of Ubeda found out that the body of Fray Juan de la Cruz had been taken from them, they were very upset. In order to get the body back, they knew that they would have to obtain special permission from a higher authority. So the leaders in the community sent special representatives to Rome to petition Pope Clement VIII to order that the body be removed from Segovia and sent back to its original burial place. Once in Rome, the leaders of this group so impressed the pope that he issued a Brief on October 15, 1596 seeking the return of the body to Ubeda. The body had been in Segovia for three years and everyone realized that any attempt to take the body back would create a serious tumult. The matter seemed to reach an impasse.

At this point, the superiors of the Discalced Carmelites intervened and came up with a compromise that they hoped would settle the affair once and for all. They proposed that Ubeda and its monastery get the remaining arm and leg of the corpse (the monastery had already retained one leg), while the monastery of Segovia would retain the head and the torso. Despite all the difficulties that the solution might entail, all parties finally agreed that this was the best answer and the dismemberment was performed.[1] Today in Segovia, high above a special altar built early in the twentieth century, one can see the ornate marble box containing the remains of Fray Juan de la Cruz.

The Beatification and Canonization Processes

Twenty-three years after the death of Fray Juan de la Cruz, the ordinary procedures to gather information for the beatification of the friar began. From 1614 to 1616, the officials gathered material in Medina del Campo, Segovia, Avila, Jean, Baeza, Ubeda, Alcaudete, and Malaga without the official intervention of Rome. Yet, it was another eleven years (1627) before the Apostolic Process that added Salamanca to its list and accepted the material gathered in the earlier process was held. In fact, the beatification did not take place until 1675 and the canonization in 1726. Many people were surprised at the long delay because they had expected the process to move as rapidly as it had for Teresa de Avila, who died in 1582 and was canonized in 1622. The question remains: "Why did it take so long?" Part of the answer lies in the conflicts between Ubeda and Segovia, in the ancient antipathy between Andalusia and Castile. Moreover, we know from Madre Ana de Jesús, the fervent disciple of Teresa and friend of Fray Juan, that some people who formed part of the leadership of the

Order still disliked Fray Juan years after his death. These people may not have been anxious to have him officially raised to the status of saint. Certainly, very serious political overtones played a role in the delay.

Furthermore, the people's almost incredible love for relics caused some problems. We have already noted how strong was the desire for relics and the miracles resulting from them in the people of Ubeda and Segovia. In 1625, the Roman authorities adamantly opposed the public veneration of people without the previous approval of Rome. On the morning of October 30, 1647, the people of Segovia and the Carmelites of the Discalced monastery there were surprised to find two official documents nailed to the doors of the Carmelite church. These documents noted that Rome had expressly forbidden the placing in a prominent place of the remains of persons having a reputation for sanctity. Furthermore, it stated that the body of Fray Juan de la Cruz was venerated in this church in such a way that contravened this regulation.[2]

The following day a letter dated October 31, 1647, from the Superior General of the Order, Fray Juan Bautista, ordered Padre Fray Bartolomé de Santa María, who was residing in the monastery at Segovia, to see to it that the body of Fray Juan de la Cruz was removed from its place of honor and buried in the ground as was customary. Within four days they had done the deed and they notified the bishop of the fact. Soon thereafter, an official of the diocese was sent to investigate and verify that the body had actually been removed and buried in accord with the Roman decree. When he had confirmed the fact, the officials in Rome were notified in the hopes that the prompt obedience of the Discalced would avoid the complete breakdown of the beatification process implied in the documents posted on the church doors. For the next year or so, the Discalced Carmelites tried to get the beatification process underway once more. Rome moved very slowly and it was necessary to proceed step by step. Finally, in 1649, the Discalced convinced Pope Innocent X to intervene and push the process ahead. Only the personal intervention of King Felipe IV of Spain accomplished this. The political route had unblocked the path and now the process began to go forward with surprising rapidity.

On February 21, 1650, a large group of well-known and trusted people, especially selected because of their credibility, arrived at the Segovian monastery of the Discalced to view the place where Fray Juan's body had been interred. They wanted to determine whether a public cult was going on around his body. A document dated February 21 states that Fray Juan's resting place is under the floor of a small chapel to the right of the church as one is leaving it. Further, the group discovered no pictures of the reformer of the Carmelites and asked where they, the candles, and the other objects that had been part of the cult might be. The friars told them that in accordance with the earlier Roman decree they had removed these objects and placed them under lock and key in a secret place in the monastery. When the group asked to see the place, the friars brought them to an obscure and remote part of the monastery where investigators were able to confirm that all these objects were indeed well out of sight. Despite this, many months of further examination of witnesses was necessary. On November 26, 1650, the tribunal declared that there was no worship or special veneration of Fray Juan de la Cruz in the Carmelite church. They sent the process with all its papers to Rome on February 9, 1651.

However, one more sensitive issue remained to be resolved. This was the question of the doctrine found in the works of Fray Juan de la Cruz. Throughout the whole of the sixteenth century and into the early part of the seventeenth, the *alumbrados* movement was very strong. This spirituality went to such extremes in accenting the interior life that its followers very often regarded the liturgy and even the authority of the Church as mere externals. While Fray Juan himself placed an emphasis on inner prayer, meditation, and contemplation, he did not share the radical response of the *alumbrados* to externals such as the liturgy and to the authority of the institutional Church. In fact, he urged individuals not to be taken up with thoughts of visions, ecstasies, and the rest, which often became *the* signs of holiness for the *alumbrados*. Nonetheless, one of the last groups of radical *alumbrados* was discovered in southern Spain in the first quarter of the seventeenth century, and Fray Juan's works and those of Teresa de Avila were found in their library. The fear of mysticism and the desire to guard orthodoxy was certainly extremely strong at this time, and the discovery did not help Fray Juan's beatification process. Officials felt that it was necessary to thoroughly examine his works. Despite the statements in Fray Juan's works saying he had submitted all he wrote to the judgment of Church officials, the strong mystical dimension of his writings made him suspect.

With all of this in mind, Rome appointed a mature, respected theologian to examine Fray Juan's works. In his final decision, he noted that what was contained in the works of Fray Juan was also to be found in the Scriptures. Therefore, it would be impossible to fault this reformer of Carmel because of the totally evangelical tone and content of his work. When the report came out in August 1655, not only were his writings not condemned but they were praised for the depth and clarity they achieved in discussing such complex topics.

It seemed that all the hurdles had been overcome and the beatification could take place, but again this was not the case. It was brought to the attention of the Roman authorities (by whom, we do not know) that there was a picture of Fray Juan in the Carmelite church in Toledo that was being reproduced and sent to several countries in Europe. Would this start the process of *non-cultu* once again? The question of the veneration, which seemed to be present, had to be cleared up before the beatification could take place. Eventually, the case was investigated, found to be true, and, as in Segovia, the cult was stopped.

Nonetheless, another question about Fray Juan's possible holiness was raised and had to be settled. While Fray Juan was in jail in the monastery in Toledo, he was accused of pure stubbornness, rebellion against the authorities of the other branch of his Order, and total disobedience despite his vow. These accusations would seem to be inconsistent with a claim to "heroic" virtue. Once again, we do not know who raised this objection or why. We only know that it was raised and ultimately settled. It was concluded that Fray Juan's attitude at that time was not rebellious (as at first it might have seemed), because he was working under the assumption that he had obeyed a higher authority: the papal legate.

Then the question of certain miracles and apparitions that took place after his death came up. It looked as if the beatification would never take place. Each step uncovered yet another objection until finally, the pope was asked to intervene once more. Though the pope asked that the process continue, the discussion about the beatification went on almost to the day of the actual ceremony. Ultimately, through the joint efforts of the Calced and Discalced Carmelite Orders, all the obstacles were cleared away and Fray Juan was beatified on January 25, 1675, and finally canonized a saint by Pope Benedict XIII on December 27, 1726.

Politics had slowed down the process, but very wise political moves, as well as convincing evidence, caused Fray Juan to be recognized as the deeply human and saintly man he was.

Segovia and Ubeda Today

Today the two cities of Segovia and Ubeda, which figured so prominently in the life and death of Fray Juan de la Cruz, are centers where his spirit still lives. The ancient stone walls and houses here bear the mark of his presence. Amid the splendor of palaces and monuments to other times sit the two monasteries where he lived, died, and was buried. Within their walls are housed objects that remind the visitor of this great Spanish mystic whose influence is intensifying in this technological age, which seems so radically different from sixteenth-century Spain.

Segovia, a short drive northwest of the bustling city of Madrid, draws thousands of tourists yearly. They come to see the ancient Roman aqueduct, the spire-topped Cathedral, and the palace of the Alcazar. Very few tourists realize as they look down the precipice from the Alcazar into the gorge below—where the Eresma ever flows beneath the black poplars reaching skyward—that just beyond them is the Discalced Carmelite monastery. Their eyes take in a pastoral scene of green rolling hills broken only by three buildings: to the right is the expansive Monastery del Parral; in the middle is the striking, though much smaller Church of the Vera Cruz; and to the left the Monastery de San Juan, a maze of interconnected buildings with the inner square cloister clearly visible. If time allows, the visitor will go to see the Monastery del Parral and the Church of the Vera Cruz, to which all tourist leaflets draw attention, but he or she is not likely to go to the nondescript monastery in which Fray Juan lived, thus bypassing a remarkable place of beauty.

As one approaches the Carmelite monastery by walking down the steep hill and crossing the Eresma River, the silence, broken only by the rushing sound of the river, is in sharp contrast to the noise of the city that can now be seen high above on the rocky cliffs. The monastery complex, with its weathered light-brown stone, is composed of the main church to the left and the monastery building and the Centro de San Juan de la Cruz to the right. The exterior is plain, but the marks of the restoration completed in 1977 are evident.

Before 1975, the monastery that had once housed as many as thirty friars, and more in centuries past, contained a handful of Carmelites in a run-down building. The inner cloister had been walled up and the garden it surrounded had been allowed to run wild. Heat and lighting were poor and dampness seeped through the extremely thick walls causing the paint to peel. A small cluttered room held some objects connected with the famous friar of the Discalced. The main church remained as it had been since the early 1930s when Fray Juan's body had been placed in an ornate monument in the side chapel. Through a back exit one could enter the monastery garden which rose rather steeply to the cliffs and caves where he had spent time in solitude. Tall grass and weeds overran the few flowers, which tried to push their way through the choking brush.

Today the monastery, still run by the Discalced, has changed. Around 1975, after months of discussion with the historical monument preservation officials, the work of restoring and renovating the building began.[3] The results are a tribute to the devotion of the Discalced and the sense of beauty which inspired them. The walls that blocked the open cloisters were removed and a large sitting room covered with a giant skylight was built on the site of what used to be the cloistered garden. The original monastic cells along two sides of the cloister were restored and modernized to provide simple but comfortable places for friars and visitors to rest and reflect. Most of the larger rooms, such as the Chapter room, became light and airy conference and meeting halls or were retained as dining rooms. Objects connected with the life and times of Fray Juan de la Cruz were artistically placed throughout the monastery to create a harmonious ensemble of modern architecture and old *objets d'art*. Two examples of these art pieces are especially striking. A brick wall forms the background for the remains of an altarpiece from the Carmel in Medina del Campo where Fray Juan had celebrated the Eucharist. Nearby, ensconced in a wall, sits a beautiful white alabaster Madonna gently lit from behind to illuminate its detail. Everything contributes to an atmosphere of simple beauty that enhances what is called El Centro de San Juan de la Cruz—a retreat and renewal center for reflection, prayer, and growth in the spirit of the reformer of Carmel. The whole monastery complex has become a living monument to Fray Juan de la Cruz.[4]

Today Ubeda, with a population of some 32,000 people, lies in the heart of Andalusia, about 320 kilometers south of Madrid. Not as famous as Segovia, and off the beaten road between Madrid and Granada, fewer visitors come to see this remarkable town situated on a sloping hillside. Ubeda is a maze of narrow streets that suddenly open into plazas containing historical buildings, such as the Palacio de las Cadenas and the Sacra Capilla del Salvador among many others. If one walks southward down the narrow, sloping street called Mortiel, past gray stone buildings from a much earlier time that huddle right on the sidewalk, one enters the plaza dominated by the Church of San Pablo. Continuing for a short distance east on the street of San Juan de la Cruz, one arrives at the Oratory of San Juan de la Cruz, an unpretentious structure built of the same gray stone that seems to have been the common material for the construction of buildings here in the seventeenth century.

Though the oratory was built in 1627, some thirty-six years after Fray Juan's death, it is connected to the original monastery founded there by the Discalced in 1587. The choir loft of the oratory is in fact the room where Fray Juan died on December 14, 1591. One reaches the loft through a series of narrow corridors in the adjoining monastery. Passing through a low door, one enters the tiny room that contains the table on which his body lay for a few hours after his death. On this table is a reliquary containing the leg and hand of Fray Juan de la Cruz, given to Ubeda after his body was taken to

Segovia. Looking down from the loft into the chapel, one sees a catafalque in the main aisle of the chapel on which rests a life-sized statue of Fray Juan reclining in death. This statue has been placed over the original burial place of the frail friar of the Reform. The Discalced Friars, who still maintain the monastery and the Oratory, have a small museum dedicated to Fray Juan in renovated rooms of the old monastery.

Though the dark, somber halls and rooms of this monastery stand in stark contrast to the light and simple beauty of the one in Segovia, the visitor nonetheless senses the spirit of the last days of Fray Juan. Leaving these dark halls to go outside and turning left to walk down the street, just behind the monastery filled with groves of olive trees, one sees those lonely plains stretching far below and somehow knows that here, too, still lives part of Fray Juan.

The Sanctity of Fray Juan de la Cruz

When Fray Juan wrote: "When evening comes, you will be examined in love,"[5] he gave his readers the key to unlock the mystery of sanctity for his time and for our own. Having immersed himself in the Scriptures, he saw the command to love as the fundamental, radical call, which God makes to every human being. To love God is to love one's neighbor, one's fellow human beings. The asceticism which Fray Juan demands is to be found within the very structure of incarnating that love. Isaiah eloquently expresses the Word of Yahweh in this regard when he says:

> "Why do we fast, but you do not see? Why humble
> ourselves, but you do not notice?" Look, you serve

your own interest on your fast day, and oppress all your workers. Look, you fast only to quarrel and to fight and to strike with a wicked fist. Such fasting as you do today will not make your voice heard on high. Is such the fast that I choose, a day to humble oneself? Is it to bow down the head like a bulrush, and to lie in sackcloth and ashes? Will you call this a fast, a day acceptable to the LORD? Is not this the fast that I choose: to loose the bonds of injustice, to undo the thongs of the yoke, to let the oppressed go free, and to break every yoke? Is it not to share your bread with the hungry, and bring the homeless poor into your house; when you see the naked, to cover them, and not to hide yourself from your own kin? Then your light shall break forth like the dawn, and your healing shall spring up quickly; your vindicator shall go before you, the glory of the LORD shall be your rear guard. Then you shall call, and the LORD will answer; you shall cry for help, and he will say, Here I am. If you remove the yoke from among you, the pointing of the finger, the speaking of evil, if you offer your food to the hungry and satisfy the needs of the afflicted, then your light shall rise in the darkness and your gloom be like the noonday. The LORD will guide you continually, and satisfy your needs in parched places, and make your bones strong; and you shall be like a watered garden, like a spring of water, whose waters never fail (58:3–11).[6]

It was precisely because Jesus did this that he shocked and scandalized the "saints" of his time. And in freeing the oppressed, he established for his disciples a charter of love, a love and compassion in and through which God the Father reaches out to all, especially to the non-persons, the ones who do not count in our society. Today our growing consciousness of the absolute need for us as Jesus' disciples to be with and concerned concretely and effectively for the non-person is yet another sign of what it is to be today's saint. Fray Juan himself, though living in another time and culture, is a model of that holiness, that wholeness brought about by and in the Spirit who teaches all things (cf. Jn 14:26).

No characteristic better describes the life and personality of Fray Juan de la Cruz than this love. He loved the poor, those oppressed by material and spiritual needs. Think of him nursing the sick in Las Bubas in Medina del Campo. His patients were those without money, the outcasts of society because of their illness and their poverty. And they held a very special place in his heart and in his loving compassion. One need but remember the friars and lay people he personally ministered to during the famine in Granada and the plague in Baeza. Then there were the children of the poor who lived in the huts surrounding his own in the encampment around the Encarnación in Avila. He taught them and loved them. He even called his brother Francisco "the greatest treasure he had on earth." He loved and showed his love for this man even though the society of his time said he should rather hide him away. He loved his brother with an "attachment" despite the conventions governing all social conduct in that Segovian period. The expectations of society were of no interest to Fray Juan because he based his life upon the command of the Master who had become his companion and friend. In short, deep human love was the foundation for all his sensitive and compassionate interrelationships.

Over his lifetime, Fray Juan became like the burning log, which is continuously attacked by the fire of Love, who is the Spirit, until finally the flame and the log become indistinguishable. That love was a love of God he encountered in all people: his mother and brother, friends like Madre Ana de Jesús, Dr. Becerra of Baeza, and Dr. Villegas of Segovia. He loved all people deeply and intimately: saint and sinner, high and low, rich and poor, for they were, like him, part of God's creation and the objects of Divine Love. Fray Juan expressed and incarnated that Love.

Moreover, he loved the whole of creation. He had to love it because of God's love for it. Through God, he loved it all, which meant he truly saw that it was good. The way of denial, which Fray Juan teaches in his works, is but a technique to free the lover in each human being. By learning to let go and to allow the world and fellow human beings to be who and what they truly are, a disciple frees her or himself to love—to the death. Those who see him and his way to Nothing (Nada) as being aloof and despising the world have totally missed the significance of Fray Juan de la Cruz.

Fray Juan's extraordinary delight in creation was the source of his strength. His gentleness and compassion was not weakness and failure. Instead, these qualities were grounded in Love and gave him the strength to be faithful to his commitments and to live every aspect of his day-to-day life fully. His experience of imprisonment in Toledo, the demands of his positions in the Order, his removal from all authority in 1591, his suffering of the malicious inquest into his past, his sympathetic understanding of the Prior's harsh and cruel treatment in Ubeda, and his painful death did not destroy his life, but all of this, and his joys, created *his* life. His holiness was not something he was born with, nor was it a sudden infusion of grace that turned him around completely. Rather, his holiness, his wholeness grew through all of his life experiences, and God's love reached others through him in the midst of these events right up to the very end of his life.

By living life fully, Fray Juan de la Cruz challenged the evils of his society and built up the good. Creation was not something apart from him; he was no angel in disguise. He was fully human, living his life in this world—and this was the life of God because he was rooted in God's creation. Because of all of this, he is San Juan de la Cruz.

Appendices

APPENDIX A

How to Read the Works of Fray Juan de la Cruz

Whenever we attempt to read the works of an author from another era—and more so when that author is a mystic—we must approach her or him with care and attention. This is surely the situation when we speak of the works of Fray Juan de la Cruz. The richness of his thought, which flows from his intimacy with God, has much to offer us today. His insights into the more difficult times experienced in every human life provide us with a way to hope. To come to a deeper appreciation of all he offers to the People of God today,[1] in reading Fray Juan's writings we might wish to keep the following points in mind.

Read Fray Juan's Works in a Particular Order

I would suggest that there is a benefit to reading Fray Juan's works in a particular order. You should begin with his poetry. In allowing him to transport you into his poetic vision of God and life, you will come to the very heart of Fray Juan. Then you would do well to read his prose works: first, *The Living Flame of Love* (preferably Redaction B, which is the one Kavanaugh has translated in his edition of the complete works of St. John of the Cross). Afterward you could proceed to *The Spiritual Canticle-B* before reading *The Ascent of Mount Carmel* and *The Dark Night*, and then the remainder of his works in the light of these works.

Keep in Mind Fray Juan's Life Experiences

It is important that you keep the life of Fray Juan de la Cruz in the forefront as you read his works. As we have seen, he loved people deeply. Keep in mind how he related to his mother and elder brother, to say nothing of his female and male friends both within and outside the Discalced Carmelite Order. His love of beauty in creation and his passionate expression of this beauty in his poetry demonstrate that his way was not a denial but an affirmation of God's gifts in life. Remembering all of this will help you to understand what he is talking about when he *seems* to be advocating their denial. Read Fray Juan's works through the prism of his life.

Understand the Special Meaning of Certain Words

It is important to understand that some words and phrases have special meanings for Fray Juan. For example, when he uses the word "soul," he is referring to the "person," the body-spirit-psyche composite, and not just to the spirit element. When he does mean "spirit" it is clear from his context. By keeping in mind this notion of "soul" as meaning "person," it is possible to avoid a false dualistic interpretation of his works. It is also important to remember his distinction of "attachment" and "detachment." For Fray Juan, "attachment" means being controlled by things and "detachment" means freedom from that control. To let go of attachment is to be free (detachment).

Be Aware of the Combination of Experiences

As he writes, Fray Juan often combines not only his experience, but also the experiences of people he came to know as they journeyed toward God. This is particularly the case when he describes the dark nights. He did this so that he might provide each reader with something with which she or he could identify. This does not mean that everything that Fray Juan describes will necessarily be a part of every individual's experience. Bearing this fact in mind will prevent a gross interpretation of Fray Juan.

Bear in Mind Fray Juan's Pedagogical Method

Fray Juan's presentations of the dark nights seem to indicate that one follows the other in a linear way, but this is a pedagogical presentation. Remember that different aspects of the personality are going through different nights (letting go, being freed) at different times. Yet, at times there may be a preponderance of one over the others, which is especially true in the passive night of the soul.

Personal Experience Plays a Role

Because Fray Juan wrote from his own experience and from the experiences of those he knew, everyone will understand Fray Juan de la Cruz more deeply in proportion to his or her personal experience of intimacy with God. And this is a lifetime process. Hence, you cannot expect to understand everything all at once. You will discover new things as you read and reread Fray Juan at different times in your life. There will be deeper insights. Fray Juan does not just communicate some intellectual knowledge, but an experience of the Sacred, of the Living God. Approach his works as if looking into a person's life with God—Father, Son, and Spirit.

A Meditative Approach

As you read Fray Juan, it is good to allow yourself to be drawn by those things that strike you most. If a particular phrase, word, or paragraph seems to draw you more, then simply stop reading and allow that particular reality to sink deeply into who you are at that moment. Mull it over—perhaps in total silence—allowing it to work its gift in your heart.

Reading these remembrances of a life with God, you will find things that you can readily understand and make your own. You will also find things that you do not understand at all. Let those go and remain with what draws you. Over a lifetime, you will come to understand and be drawn to more and more elements of Juan's description of the journey, because those are the things that God desires for you at any given time. If in reading Fray Juan de la Cruz you find more and more a compassionate, loving, gentle God, you have truly understood this great sixteenth-century Spanish mystic.

Selected Texts from the Works of Fray Juan de la Cruz

The Major Works

THE ASCENT OF MOUNT CARMEL

This work consists of three parts: the "Sketch of Mount Carmel"; the poem "The Dark Night"; and the prose "Treatise." It is not so much a commentary as we find in some of his other works as a real treatise. "The Sketch of Mount Carmel" with its demands of the ascent written on it is most fascinating. He probably completed "The Sketch of Mount Carmel" in Beas in 1578–1579. Fray Juan wrote the poem shortly after his escape from the Toledo prison, and it bears the marks of this experience. He began the "Treatise" in El Calvario, then continued to work on it in Baeza, and finally finished it in Granada in 1584. The "Treatise" deals with the way to the highest union with God. Fray Juan accents the difficulties of the way. For him, one cannot obtain this union without passing through times of darkness and difficulties, which are purifications of the senses and the spirit. He treats of all kinds of demands and negations in the active process to union with God. Many of these things, while important for the sixteenth-century Spaniard, have perhaps even more meaning for believers today. For in this process of letting go, one lives the divine life more and more fully as one lives more and more simply. Strangely, the "Treatise" ends rather abruptly.

THE SOUL WILL BE CLOTHED IN GOD, in a new understanding of God in God...and in a new love of God in God, once the will is stripped of all the cravings and satisfactions. And God will vest the soul with new knowledge when the other old ideas and images are cast aside [Col 3:9]...As a result one's activities, once human, now become divine.

The Ascent of Mount Carmel I, 5. 7 (Kav. p. 129)

THE MOMENT IT RECOLLECTS ITSELF in the presence of God, it enters into an act of general, loving, peaceful and tranquil knowledge, drinking wisdom and love and delight.

The Ascent of Mount Carmel II, 14, 2 (Kav. p. 192)

IF I HAVE ALREADY TOLD YOU ALL THINGS in My Word, My Son, and if I have no other word, what answer or revelation can I now make that would surpass this? Fasten your eyes on him alone, because in him I have spoken and revealed all, and in him you will discover even more than you ask for and desire.... For he is my entire locution and response, vision and revelation, which I have already spoken, answered, manifested, and revealed to you, by giving him to you as a brother, companion, master, ransom, and reward.

The Ascent of Mount Carmel II, 22, 5 (Kav. pp. 230–231)

THEY OBTAIN MORE JOY and recreation in creatures through the dispossession of them. They cannot rejoice in them if they behold them with possessiveness, for this is a care that, like a trap, holds the spirit to earth and does not allow wideness of heart [2 Cor 6:11].

The Ascent of Mount Carmel III, 20, 2 (Kav. p. 302)

THE DARK NIGHT

This prose work is more truly a commentary on the poem and was most likely finished around 1584–1586. Here Fray Juan covers in more detail the passive nights involved in the journey to God. For him, the human being needs to be transformed in his or her whole reality. This means that the composite, the person must learn to be free both in body (senses) and psyche (spirit). To discuss how God transforms the person, he uses the image of the passive nights of the senses and the spirit. In this commentary, he shows how both these nights are extremely difficult (particularly the night of the spirit), and how one should respond to these dark contexts of life with God. These periods of letting go are found in each human being's life as the believer moves more and more deeply into God. Hence, this work of Fray Juan is very useful in our understanding of the process.

IT SHOULD BE KNOWN, then, that God nurtures and caresses the soul, after it has been resolutely converted to his service, like a loving mother who warms her child with the heat of her bosom, nurses it with good milk and tender food, and carries and caresses it in her arms. But as the child grows older, the mother withholds her caresses and hides her tender love; she rubs bitter aloes on her sweet breast and sets the child down from her arms, letting it walk on its own feet so that it may put aside the habits of childhood and grow accustomed to greater and more important things.

The Dark Night I, l, 2 (Kav. p. 361)

FOR CONTEMPLATION IS NOTHING ELSE than a secret and peaceful and loving inflow of God, which, if not hampered, fires the soul in the spirit of love....

The Dark Night I, 10, 6 (Kav. p. 382)

SOFTENED AND HUMBLED BY ARIDITIES and hardships and by other temptations and trials in which God exercises the soul in the course of this night, individuals become meek toward God and themselves, and also toward their neighbor. As a result, they no longer become impatiently angry with themselves and their faults, or with their neighbor's; neither are they displeased or disrespectfully querulous with God for not making them perfect quickly.

The Dark Night I, 13, 7 (Kav. pp. 390–391)

IT REMAINS TO BE SAID, then, that even though this happy night darkens the spirit, it does so only to impart light concerning all things; and even though it humbles individuals and reveals their miseries, it does so only to exalt them; and even though it impoverishes and empties them of all possessions and natural affection, it does so only that they may reach out divinely to the enjoyment of all earthly and heavenly things, with a general freedom of spirit in them all.

The Dark Night II, 9, 1 (Kav. p. 412)

THE SPIRITUAL CANTICLE

Thirty-one stanzas of the poem were written while Fray Juan was in the prison cell in Toledo (1577–1578). Fray Juan wrote the next three stanzas when he was Rector in Baeza (1579–1581), and the last five were composed between 1582–1584. He based the poem on the *Song of Songs,* which provided him with much solace in prison. Fray Juan wrote the first commentary in 1584, and composed the second redaction some years later. Both the poem and commentary deal with the whole journey to God through the classical stages: Purgative, Illuminative, and Unitive. In it Fray Juan describes the anguish of the person (the Bride) who leaves behind everything to pursue the Son of God (the Bridegroom), then the joy of finding and being found by God, and, ultimately, the intensifying wonder and passion of being taken by God into full union with the Trinity here and now in this life. This is a very passionate piece, which does not shrink from expressing the intimacy of God and the person.

SINCE THE DESIRE IN WHICH SHE SEEKS HIM is authentic and her love intense, she does not want to leave any possible means untried. The soul that truly loves God is not slothful in doing all she can to find the Son of God, her Beloved. Even after she has done everything, she is dissatisfied and thinks she has done nothing.

The Spiritual Canticle 3, 1 (Kav. p. 490)

AND IN THIS ELEVATION OF ALL THINGS through the Incarnation of his Son and through the glory of his resurrection according to the flesh, not only did the Father beautify creatures partially, but rather we can say, he clothed them entirely in beauty and dignity.

The Spiritual Canticle 5, 4 (Kav. p. 497)

IT SHOULD BE KNOWN THAT LOVE never reaches perfection until lovers are so alike that one is transfigured in the other.

The Spiritual Canticle 11, 12 (Kav. p. 515)

LOVE PRODUCES SUCH LIKENESS in this transformation of lovers that one can say each is the other and both are one. The reason is that in the union and transformation of love each gives possession of self to the other, and each leaves and exchanges self for the other. Thus each one lives in the other and is the other and both are one in the transformation of love.

The Spiritual Canticle 12, 7 (Kav. p. 518)

SO CREATURES WILL BE FOR THE SOUL a harmonious symphony of sublime music surpassing all concerts and melodies of the world.... Accordingly, she says that her Beloved is silent music because in him she knows and enjoys this symphony of spiritual music.

The Spiritual Canticle 14–15, 25 (Kav. p. 536)

IN THIS SAME WAY THE SOUL PERCEIVES in that tranquil wisdom that all creatures, higher and lower ones alike, according to what each in itself has received from God, raise their voice in testimony to what God is. She beholds that each in its own way, bearing God within itself according to its capacity, magnifies God. And, thus, all these voices form one voice of music praising the grandeur, wisdom, and wonderful knowledge of God.

The Spiritual Canticle 14–15, 27 (Kav. p. 536)

Because God vitally transforms the soul into him-
self, all these faculties, appetites, and movements lose their natural imperfection and are changed to divine.

The Spiritual Canticle 20–21, 4 (Kav. p. 553)

The union wrought between the two natures and
the communication of the divine to the human in this state is
such that even though neither changes its being, both appear
to be God.

The Spiritual Canticle 22, 4 (Kav. p. 561)

THE LIVING FLAME OF LOVE

Fray Juan wrote the commentary on his poem for his
friend Doña Ana de Peñalosa. He did this in about two weeks
(1586). However, he reworked it a few months before he died
in 1591. Though there are no substantial changes, it is a final tes-
tament, which Fray Juan de la Cruz wished to give. Moreover,
some of the additions to the second redaction clearly accent
positive points, which were dear to the heart of Fray Juan. The
whole work focuses on living the divine life that is a gift, and
the wonderful experience that it is. For Fray Juan, living the
divine life is the Trinity's gift to all who dare to love. That divine
life is lived in the human life of each believer here and now. The
intensification of this life creates a whole context of incredibly
powerful passion and desire for total union. In this commentary,
Fray Juan describes the wonder and the happiness of this life
lived with God here and now. It has a powerful summary of the
purgation process (stanza I, 19–25), which is extremely striking
when one considers the particular selection of words and scrip-

tural quotations Fray Juan uses. There is also a long digression on spiritual directors (stanza III), who Fray Juan believed were hindering the work of God who desires to bring people to deeper union with Father, Son, and Spirit. Here we find Fray Juan's principle of spiritual guidance: enable the person to hear the voice of the Spirit and empower her or him to follow it even when that path is not the one the guide might wish.

THUS IN THIS STATE THE SOUL CANNOT make acts because the Holy Spirit makes them all and moves it toward them. As a result all the acts of the soul are divine, since the movement to these acts and their execution stems from God. It seems to such persons that every time this flame shoots up, making them love with delight and divine quality, it is giving them eternal life, since it raises them up to the activity of God in God.

The Living Flame I, 4 (Kav. p. 642)

...[I]T MAKES THE SOUL LIVE IN GOD spiritually and experience the life of God in the manner David mentions: *My heart and my flesh rejoiced in the living God* [Ps 84:2]. David did not refer to God as living because of a necessity to do so, for God is always living, but in order to manifest that the spirit and the senses, transformed in God, enjoy him in a living way, which is to taste the living God—that is, God's life, eternal life.

The Living Flame I, 6 (Kav. p. 643)

IT IS NOTEWORTHY, THEN, THAT LOVE is the inclination, strength, and power for the soul in making its way to God, for love unites it with God. The more degrees of love it has, the more deeply it enters into God and centers itself in him.

The Living Flame I, 13 (Kav. p. 645)

...[T]HE FATHER OF LIGHTS [Jas 1:17], who is not close-fisted but diffuses himself abundantly, as the sun does its rays, without being a respecter of persons [Acts 10:34], wherever there is room—always showing himself gladly along the highways and byways—does not hesitate or consider it of little import to find his delights with the children of the earth at a common table in the world [Prv. 8:31].

The Living Flame I, 15 (Kav. p. 646)

THE SOUL FEELS ITS ARDOR STRENGTHEN and increase and its love become so refined in this ardor that seemingly there flow seas of loving fire within it, reaching to the heights and depths of the earthly and heavenly spheres, imbuing all with love. It seems to it that the entire universe is a sea of love in which it is engulfed, for, conscious of the living point or center of love within itself, it is unable to catch sight of the boundaries of this love.

The Living Flame II, 10 (Kav. p. 661)

TRUE LOVERS ARE ONLY CONTENT when they employ all they are in themselves, all they are worth, have, and receive, in the beloved; and the greater all this is, the more satisfaction they receive in giving it.

The Living Flame III, 1 (Kav. p. 673)

YET GOD ALWAYS ACTS IN THIS WAY—as the soul is able to see—moving, governing, bestowing being, power, graces and gifts upon all creatures bearing them all in himself by his power, presence, and substance.

The Living Flame IV, 7 (Kav. p. 710)

THE SAYINGS OF LIGHT AND LOVE

While he was confessor at the Monastery of the Encarnación in Avila (1572–1577), Juan de la Cruz would often write small sayings on slips of paper and give them to the nuns he was directing. He took up this practice again while he was doing spiritual direction in Andalusia (1578–1588). Certainly many of these short sayings have been lost, but those that have survived tell us a great deal. The themes treat of letting go, self-denial, love as the center of a person's being and God's, the life of faith, and compassion. In short, he presented the Gospel itself very succinctly.

WELL AND GOOD IF ALL THINGS CHANGE, Lord God, provided we are rooted in you.

The Sayings of Light and Love 34 (Kav. p. 88)

WHEN FIXED ON SOMETHING ELSE, one's appetite leaves no room for the angel to move it.

The Sayings of Light and Love 38 (Kav. p. 88)

WHEN EVENING COMES, you will be examined in love. Learn to love as God desires to be loved and abandon your own ways of acting.

The Sayings of Light and Love 60 (Kav. p. 90)

THE SOUL THAT WALKS IN LOVE neither tires others nor grows tired.

The Sayings of Light and Love 97 (Kav. p. 92)

THOSE WHO DO NOT LOVE THEIR NEIGHBOR abhor God.

The Sayings of Light and Love 167 (Kav. p. 97)

Letters

While Fray Juan de la Cruz certainly wrote more than the thirty-three letters we have, we are fortunate to have these. Some of the nuns feared that the letters might be used against Fray Juan, and they destroyed many in the months just before his death. Other people who probably received letters simply never kept them after having read them and/or answered them, as was the case with Teresa. The first extant letter dates from 1581, while the last, which is only a fragment, from 1591. These letters give us some interesting insights into Fray Juan's life and work. Since there are no surviving letters to Teresa of Avila or to his family, we are missing those that would most likely provide more insight into how he felt about the Teresian Reform and about his family.

JESUS BE IN YOUR SOUL and thanks to him that he has enabled me not to forget the poor, as you say, or be idle, as you say. For it greatly vexes me to think you believe what you say; this would be very bad after so many kindnesses on your part when I least deserved them. That's all I need now is to forget you! Look, how could this be so in the case of one who is in my soul as you are?

> *Letter 19*: To Doña Juana de Pedraza in Granada. Segovia, October 12, 1589 (Kav. p. 754)

BE COURAGEOUS, MY DAUGHTER, and give yourself greatly to prayer, forgetting this thing and that, for after all we have no other good or security or comfort than this, for after having left all for God, it is right that we not long for support or comfort in anything but Him...

Letter 22: To Madre Leonor de San Gabriel, Discalced Carmelite, in Córdoba, Madrid, June or July 1590(?) (Kav. p. 758)

Poems

The incredibly marvelous verses of Fray Juan de la Cruz come from a man who suffered much and ultimately dared to rejoice in the realization that God is found not only in the light, but also in the darkness experienced in life. His poetry stems from the years 1578 to 1586. However, he wrote most of his poems either in his prison cell or shortly after his escape. Some poems were re-narrations and reconstructions of biblical stories. All of them contain the story of the person with God, and more particularly of God with the human community. In reading Fray Juan's poems and allowing oneself to be taken into the heart of the poem, one is carried into the very presence of the Divine. He wrote some poems to the tunes of popular love songs of his day so they could be sung, as they often were by his novices, as well as by Teresa of Avila and her communities.

My Beloved, the mountains,
and lonely wooded valleys,
strange islands,
and resounding rivers,

the whistling of love-stirring breezes,
the tranquil night
at the time of the rising dawn,
silent music,
sounding solitude,
the supper that refreshes, and deepens love.

The Spiritual Canticle-B, 14–15 (Kav. p. 76)

And though I suffer darknesses
in this mortal life,
that is not so hard a thing
for even if I have no light
I have the life of heaven.
For the blinder love is
the more it gives such life,
holding the soul surrendered,
living without light in darkness.

11. *Without support yet with support, living without light, in darkness,*
    I am wholly being consumed, 2 (Kav. p. 70)

He who is sick with love,
whom God himself has touched,
finds his tastes so changed
that they fall away
like a fevered man's
who loathes any food he sees
and desires I–don't–know–what
which is so gladly found.

12. *Not for all of beauty will I ever lose myself, but for I-don't-know-*
    what which is so gladly gained, 2 (Kav. p. 71)

The Virgin, weighed
with the Word of God,
comes down the road:
if only you'll shelter her.

13. Christmas Refrain (Kav. p. 73)

The Minor Works

THE PRECAUTIONS

Among his other works that we have are *The Precautions*. After his imprisonment in Toledo, Fray Juan wrote these pieces of advice for the nuns in the monastery in Beas. *The Precautions* are divided into three groups, each of which contains three precautions. The first is *Against the World* (Kav. pp.720–722), the second is *Against the Devil* (Kav. pp. 722–724), and the third is *Against Oneself and the Shrewdness of Sensuality* (Kav. p. 724). This work of Juan de la Cruz is one which should be read while keeping his own life in mind, as well as what he has said in *The Spiritual Canticle* and *The Living Flame of Love*.

THE FOUR COUNSELS TO A RELIGIOUS

Fray Juan speaks of the first counsel that he calls "resignation," which contains for him a sense of focusing on inner and external quiet. The second counsel, "mortification," brings one to see how day-to-day life begins to transform the person who allows this to happen. The third counsel, "practice of virtue," involves living for God, which is to live humanly and humanely. And the fourth counsel, "true solitude," allows everything and everyone to be as God desires.

DEGREES OF PERFECTION

These short statements are very similar to *The Sayings of Light and Love*. Each is a piece of advice to religious, who in following it will find their lives enhanced as they journey with God to that oneness Fray Juan believed was the call of all human beings.

CENSURE AND OPINIONS

While we know little about the nun who is the subject of this short piece, we do know that it concerns some seemingly unusual religious experiences she had. Fray Juan had been asked to give his opinions on her. He wrote this during his time in Segovia (1588–1591). What is important in this text is the way Fray Juan is able to synthesize norms and how to discern the things of God as found in life's experiences. We see here a man who was very understanding, yet extremely perceptive and able to get to the heart of the matter when it came to people's state on their journey to God.

APPENDIX C

For Further Reading

I HAVE LISTED BELOW some of the biographies, translations, and modern studies of Fray Juan de la Cruz that might be useful to those who desire to do further reading.

Biographies

Fray Alonso de la Madre de Dios. *Vida, virtudes y milagros del santo padre Fray Juan de la Cruz, maestro y padre de la Reforma de la Orden de los Descalzos de Nuestra Señora del Monte Carmelo.* Biblioteca Naciónal de Madrid, Ms. 13460.

> This manuscript was never published even though it was written by someone who knew Fray Juan de la Cruz personally and had been involved in gathering the material for his beatification process. Because of the personal involvement of the author, this particular work contains some details arranged in an orderly fashion that are impossible to find elsewhere.

Jean Baruzi. *Saint Jean de la Croix et le problème de l'expérience mystique.* Paris: F. Alcan, 1924.

> This work on Fray Juan is not primarily concerned with his biography, but the biographical section cited above is a superb interpretation of the life of Fray Juan. One cannot study seriously the life or work of Fray Juan without consulting this classical text.

Gerald Brenan. *St. John of the Cross: His Life & Poetry* (with a translation of the poetry by Lynda Nicholson). Cambridge: Cambridge University Press, 1973.

A short and interesting presentation of the life of Fray Juan, employing some of the more recent discoveries and leaving out some of the hagiographical material found in the works of other authors.

Fr. Bruno de Jesús-Marie, O.C.D. *Saint Jean de la Croix*. Bruges: Les Etudes Carmelitaines Chez Desclée de Brouwer, 1961 edition.

The original 1929 edition is available in English translation: Benedict Zimmerman, ed. *St. John of the Cross*. London: Sheed and Ward, 1956. The work by Father Bruno de Jesús-Marie is very interesting but highly hagiographical.

H. Chandebois. *Portrait de saint Jean de la Croix. La flûte de roseau.* Paris: Grasset, 1947.

A good work that provides the Carmelite milieu in which Fray Juan lived as well as the basic events in the life of this mystic.

Crisogono de Jesús, O.C.D. *Vida y obras completas de San Juan de la Cruz*. (Revised posthumously with critical notes by Matías del Niño Jesús and critical edition, notes and appendices by Lucinio del SS. Sacramento), 5th edition. Madrid: Biblioteca de autores cristianos, 1964.

Without a doubt, this is one of the most complete works giving the life and context of Fray Juan de la Cruz. It is of exceptional value for the scholarly material constantly employed. However, the author made no judgment as to the historical value of the incidents, which he weaves together from primary sources to form this life of Fray Juan. An English translation from the 1955 edition was done by Kathleen Pond: *The Life of St. John of the Cross*. London: Longmans, Green & Co, 1958.

Jéronimo de San José. *Historia del Venerable Padre Fray Juan de la Cruz Primer Descalzo carmelita, compañero y Coadjutor de Santa Teresa de Jesús en la Fundación de su Reforma.* Madrid, 1641.

> Recently published as Jéronimo de San José (Ezquerra), *Historia del Venerable Padre Fray Juan de la Cruz.* Nueva ed. preparada por J. V. Rodríguez. Valladolid, Junta de Castilla y León, 1993, 2 vols., 24, 5 cm.
>
> One of the earliest biographies, but filled with strong hagiographical characteristics. It is nonetheless an important source for biographical information.

José de Jesús María (Quiroga). *Historia de la vida y virtudes del Venerable P. Fray Juan de la Cruz Primer Religioso de la Reformación de los descalzos de Nuestra Señora del Carmen con Declaración de los Grados de la vita contemplativa por donde N.S. le levanto a una rara perfeción en estado de destierro. Y del singular don, que tuvo para enseñar la sabiduría divina que transforma las almas en Dios.* Brussels: Ivan de Meerbeeck, 1628.

> Recently published as José de Jesús María(Quiroga), *Historia de la vida y virtudes del venerable P. Fr. Juan de la Cruz...* Ed. de F. Antolín. Salamanca, Junta de Castilla y León, 1992, p. 618.
>
> This work is highly hagiographical and contains the usual material found in the other earlier biographies. It is especially interpretative of the life of Fray Juan within the context that José de Jesús María sees as being that of holiness. For this latter reason, it is extremely interesting to read.

Federico Ruiz, O.C.D. and others. *God Speaks in the Night: The Life, Times, and Teaching of St. John of the Cross.* [English Translation by Kieran Kavanaugh, O.C.D.] Washington, D.C.: ICS Publications, 1991.

> This is a fine collection of chapters which deal with various dimensions of Fray Juan de la Cruz' life and beautiful photographs from various locales in which he lived as well as images

of the saint. This work done by various authors provides an excellent overview of the saint and the times.

St. John of the Cross: A Digital Library, CD-Rom. Washington, D.C.: ICS Publications.

This CD contains the works of Fray Juan de la Cruz in Spanish along with the 1991 Kavanaugh/Rodriguez translation and the E. Allison Peers translation, plus the Douay-Rheims translation of the Bible from the Latin version used by Fray Juan de la Cruz. It contains superb tools for further research on various themes and the works of Fray Juan de la Cruz.

English Versions of the Works of Fray Juan de la Cruz

The Collected Works of St. John of the Cross. Revised edition. [Translated by Kieran Kavanaugh, O.C.D. and Otilio Rodriguez, O.C.D.] Washington, D.C.: ICS Publications, 1991.

John of the Cross. *The Living Flame of Love, Versions A and B.* [Translated with introduction and commentary notes by Jane Ackerman.] Binghamton, NY: Medieval & Renaissance Texts & Studies, 1995.

This is an excellent text highlighting the differences (additions and omissions) in the two versions. Dr. Ackerman has provided us all with a marvelous tool, painstakingly done. Anyone interested in a serious reading of *The Living Flame of Love* will want to have this edition at hand.

Modern Studies on St. John of the Cross

Leonard Doohan. *The Contemporary Challenge of John of the Cross: An Introduction to His Life and Teaching.* Washington, D.C.: ICS Publications, 1995.

A very fine introduction of Fray Juan de la Cruz for the contemporary reader.

Kieran Kavanaugh, O.C.D. *John of the Cross: Doctor of Light and Love.* New York: The Crossroad Publishing Company, 1999.

This is a very good presentation of the life and works of Fray Juan de la Cruz done by an eminent translator and scholar of the sanjuanist tradition.

Iain Matthew, O.C.D. *The Impact of God: Soundings from St. John of the Cross.* London: Hodder & Stoughton, 1995.

This short book offers an excellent interpretation of the meaning of Fray Juan de la Cruz and his works for today's journey to God.

Antonio T. de Nicolás. *St. John of the Cross: Alchemist of the Soul.* New York: Paragon House, 1989.

With a very brief view of his life and bilingual edition of the poetry, this book provides the reader with some interesting perspectives on the work of Fray Juan de la Cruz.

Wilfrid McGreal, O.Carm., *At the Fountain of Elijah: The Carmelite Tradition* [Traditions of Christian Spirituality Series]. London: Darton, Longman & Todd, 1999.

Provides an excellent, readable view of the Carmelite tradition in which Fray Juan de la Cruz is inserted.

Steven Payne, O.C.D., ed. *Carmelite Studies VI. John of the Cross: Conferences & Essays by Members of the Institute of Carmelite Studies, and Others.* Washington, D.C.: ICS Publications, 1995.

This book contains some very excellent articles dealing with various dimensions of the teaching and impact of Fray Juan de la Cruz today.

John Welch, O. Carm. *The Carmelite Way: An Ancient Path for Today's Pilgrim.* Mahwah, NJ: Paulist Press, 1996.

> While not directly on St. John of the Cross' approach, this book gives a marvelous introduction to the Carmelite path to God—a path inspired greatly by Fray Juan de la Cruz.

John Welch, O. Carm. *When Gods Die: An Introduction to John of the Cross.* New York/Mahwah, NJ: Paulist Press, 1990.

> An excellent book for those who wish to delve more deeply into the ideas and teachings of Fray Juan de la Cruz.

Endnotes

Introduction

1. Richard P. Hardy, *Search for Nothing: The Life of John of the Cross* (New York, NY: Crossroad, 1982).

2. Jean Baruzi, *Saint Jean de la Croix et le problème de l'expérience mystique* (Paris: Librarie Félix Alcan, 1924).

3. Crisogono de Jesús, O.C.D., *Vida y Obras de San Juan de la Cruz* (Textual revisions and critical notes by Matías del Niño Jesus, O.C.D. and critical edition of the works by Lucinio del SS. Sacramento, O.C.D.), (Madrid: Biblioteca de Autores Cristianos, 1964). (Hereafter this work is referred to as BAC.) This life is certainly extremely well done and provides an excellent setting for Fray Juan de la Cruz. However, the author does not seem to have always judiciously selected the more reliable witnesses and documents upon which to base his story. The other major biography in our century is that of Bruno de Jésus-Marie, *Saint Jean de la Croix* (Bruge: Desclée de Brouwer, 1961). Even more complete than these, though done by a team of scholars, is the work of Federico Ruiz, ed., and others, *God Speaks in the Night: The Life, Times, and Teaching of St. John of the Cross* [Translated by Kieran Kavanaugh, O.C.D.] (Washington, D.C.: ICS Publications, 1991). This is certainly a very fine source of information on the life and work of Fray Juan de la Cruz.

Chapter 1

1. Jose Gomez-Menor Fuentes, *El linaje familias de santa Teresa y de san Juan de la Cruz: sus parrentes toledanos* (Toledo: 1970), pp. 22–67. In this period, even if it was not absolutely necessary to hide one's Jewish ancestry, because of the religious and social restrictions that this would place upon any of the descendants, it was wise to do so. For more detailed descriptions of the situation, see also Stephen Clissold, *St. Teresa of Avila* (London: Sheldon Press, 1979), pp. 1–13;

Teofanes Egido, "The Historical Setting of St. Teresa's Life" in *Carmelite Studies* I (1981), pp. 122–182.

2. Jose Gomez-Menor Fuentes, El linaje familias de santa Teresa y de san Juan de la Cruz: sus parrentes toledanos (Toledo: 1970), p. 43.

3. Jeronimo de San José, Historia del Venerable Padre Fray Juan de la Cruz primer Descalzo carmelita, compañero y Coadjutor de Santa Teresa de Jesús en la Fundación de su Reforma (Madrid: Diego Diaz de la Carrera, 1641), p. 12. The date is uncertain. He might have been born either on the feast of John the Baptist in June or on the feast of John the Evangelist in December. This specification of the feast day is deduced from the fact that his name was Juan and that he might have been given the name because of the feast day on which he was born, as was common at that time. Unfortunately, a fire in the parish church destroyed the records of his baptism.

4. Living Flame of Love-B, 1, Crisogono de Jesús, O.C.D., Vida y Obras de San Juan de la Cruz (Revision and notes by Matías del Niño Jesús, O.C.D.; critical edition by Lucinio del SS. Sacramento, O.C.D.) (Madrid: Biblioteca de Autores Cristianos [BAC], 1964), p. 829. The English translation is from The Collected Works of St. John of the Cross, translated by Kieran Kavanaugh, O.C.D., and Otilio Rodriguez, O.C.D., with Revisions and Introductions by Kieran Kavanaugh, O.C.D. (Washington, D.C.: Institute of Carmelite Studies Publications, 1991), p. 52. Hereafter, The Collected Works is referred to as (Kav.). One might also wonder if the various colors referred to in The Spiritual Canticle are not the result of a trained weaver's sensitivity to color combinations.

5. Fray José de Velasco, Vida y virtudes y muerte del Venerable Varon Francisco de Yepes, Vezino de Medina del Campo, que murió M. DC., VII (Barcelona: G. Margarit, 1624), p. 7.

6. Biblioteca Nacional de Madrid (BNM), Ms. 12758, fol. 613.

7. Martín Alberto Marcos, "El sistema hospitalerio de Medina del Campo en el siglo XVI" in Cuadernos de Investigación Historica, 2 (1978), pp. 349-351.

8. Jeronimo de San José, *Historia*, pp. 23–24.

9. Martín Alberto Marcos, "El sistema hospitalerio," p. 348.

10. Crisogono de Jesús, O.C.D., *Vida y Obras*, p. 45.

Chapter 2

1. *The Shepherd Boy,* BAC, p. 943 (Kav., pp. 57–58).

2. Crisogono de Jesús, *Vida y Obras*, p. 49.

3. Teresa de Jesus, *The Book of Her Foundations*, chapter 3, 15–16 in Kieran Kavanaugh, O.C.D. and Otilio Rodriguez, O.C.D. translators, *The Collected Works of St. Teresa of Avila,* vol. III (Washington, D.C.: ICS Publications, 1985) pp. 111–112.

4. Fray John of the Cross was known at this time as Fray Juan de Santo Matía. Cf. Teresa de Jesus, *The Book of Her Foundations*, chapter III, 17, Kav., p. 112.

5. Fray Juan was to be her defender constantly throughout his lifetime. Even after Teresa's death, Fray Juan de la Cruz sided with Madre Ana de Jesús for the more humanitarian and Teresian inspiration of the Rule's interpretation against Padre Doria (cf. Ildefonso Moriones, *Ana de Jesús y la herencía teresiana. Humanismo cristiano o rigor primitivo?* Rome: Edizioni del Teresianum, 1968). He would seek her help and advice many times about the establishment of the Reform. Moreover, he was to be totally faithful to the Reform as she wanted and conceived it. Nonetheless, he knew how to moderate some of Teresa's ideas and approaches.

6. See also Efren de la Madre de Dios and Otger Steggink, eds., *Obras Completas de Santa Teresa de Jesús* (Madrid: Biblioteca de Autores Cristianos, 1967). Epistolario, Carta a D. Francisco de Salcedo, Avila. Carta 13, 2, p. 677. See the English translation by Kieran Kavanaugh, O.C.D., *The Collected Letters of St. Teresa of Avila* (Washington, D.C.: ICS Publications, 2001), p. 60. For a very fine discussion of the relationship of Madre Teresa de Jesús and Fray Juan de la Cruz, see also G. Morel, *Le sens de l'existence selon s. Jean de la Croix* (Paris: Aubier, 1961), pp. 78–97.

7. Teresa de Jesús, *The Book of Her Foundations*, chapter 13, 3 (Kav., pp. 161–162).

8. Fray Alonso de la Madre de Dios, *Vida, virtudes y milagros del santo padre Fray Juan de la Cruz, maestro y padre de la Reforma de la Orden de los Descalzos de Nuestra Señora del Monte Carmelo* (Biblioteca Nacional de Madrid [BNM], Ms. 13460), fols. 23–24.

9. Teresa de Jesús, *The Book of Her Foundations*, chapter 14, 6–7 (Kav., pp. 165–166).

10. See also BNM, Ms. 8568, fol. 371, quoted by José Gomez-Menor Fuentes, *El linaje familias*, p. 13.

11. This love that Fray Juan had for his mother and brother must be kept in mind as we read his words, particularly the following passage: "...you should have an equal love for and an equal forgetfulness of all persons, whether relatives or not, and withdraw your heart from relatives as much as from others, and in some ways even more for fear that flesh and blood might be quickened by the natural love which is ever alive among kin and which must always be mortified for the sake of spiritual perfection." *The Precautions*, 5, BAC, p. 948 (Kav., p. 720).

12. José de Velasco, *Vida, virtudes y muerte del Venerable Varon Francisco,* p. 88.

13. Very likely on some such occasion he would have spoken to them words similar to what he wrote in *The Ascent of Mount Carmel:* "Those who now desire to question God or receive some vision or revelation are guilty not only of foolish behavior but also of offending him, by not fixing his eyes entirely upon Christ and by living with the desire for some other novelty. God could respond as follows: 'If I have already told you all things in my Word, my Son, and if I have no other word, what answer or revelation can I now make that would surpass this? Fasten your eyes on him alone, because in him I have spoken and revealed all, and in him you will discover even more than you ask for and desire'" (*The Ascent* II, 22, 5, BAC, pp. 450–451, Kav., pp. 230–231).

It is indeed unfortunate that we do not have copies of the sermons he gave during this time, but perhaps some things which have come to us as his maxims might have been the original foundation for some of these homilies that touched the people of the villages so deeply. For example: "Let your speech be such that no one may be offended, and let it concern things which would not cause you regret were all to know of them" (*Maxims*, n. 150, BAC, p. 969; *The Sayings of Light and Love,* Kav., n. 151, p. 96). "Whoever knows how to die in all will have life in all" (*Other Counsels*, BAC, n. 169, p. 970; *The Sayings of Light and Love,* Kav., n. 160, p. 97). "Anyone who complains or grumbles is not perfect, nor is he even a good Christian" (*Other Counsels,* BAC, n. 171, p. 970; *The Sayings of Light and Love,* Kav., n. 162, p. 97).

14. Alonso de la Madre de Dios, *Vida, virtudes,* I, 18 and 20, fols. 62 and 70.

Chapter 3

1. Nicolas González y González, *El Monasterio de la Encarnación de Avila*, vol. I (Avila: Caja Central de Ahorros y Prestamos de Avila, 1976), pp. 295–302.

2. *Maxims*, BAC, n. 157, p. 969 (*The Sayings of Light and Love,* Kav., n. 158, p. 97).

3. *Maxims*, BAC, n. 154, p. 969 (*The Sayings of Light and Love,* Kav., n. 155, p. 96).

4. *Maxims*, BAC, n. 152, p. 969 (*The Sayings of Light and Love,* Kav., n. 153, p. 96).

5. Nicolas González y González, *El Monasterio,* p. 312.

6. *The Sayings of Light and Love,* BAC, n. 59, p. 965 (Kav., n. 60, p. 90).

7. Silverio de Santa Teresa, O.C.D., ed., *Obras de San Juan de la Cruz, Doctor de la Iglesia* (Biblioteca Mistica Carmelitana [hereafter referred to as BMC], Burgos: Tipografia de "El Monte Carmelo," 1931). Relación de Fray Juan Evangelista, vol. 13, p. 389 (BNM Ms. 12738, ca.

fol. 559). Since the editor does not give the ms. pages in the printed text, I attempt to give the approximate folio number in parentheses.

    8. Crisogono de Jesús, *Vida y Obras*, pp. 84–85.

Chapter 4

    1. *Obras Completas de Santa Teresa de Jesús*, carta 218, p. 879; *The Collected Letters of St. Teresa of Avila* [Translated by Kieran Kavanaugh, O.C.D.] (Washington, D.C.: ICS Publications, 2001), Letter 218, (Kav., pp. 578–581).

    2. *Obras Completas de Santa Teresa de Jesús*, carta 218, p. 880; *The Collected Letters of St. Teresa of Avila,* Letter 218, 6 (Kav., p. 580).

    3. *Living Flame of Love-B* 1, 19–20, BAC, p. 838 (Kav., pp. 648–649).

    4. *A Romance on the Psalm "By the Waters of Babylon"* (Ps 136), BAC, 939–940 (Kav., pp. 68–69).

    5. BNM, Ms. 12738, fol. 138.

    6. Alonso de la Madre de Dios: *Vida, Virtudes*, BNM, Ms. 13460, fol. 126.

    7. BNM, Ms. 12738, fol. 386.

Chapter 5

    1. Though most scholars maintain that Fray Juan de la Cruz attended this meeting, the study of P. Hipolito de la Sagrada Familia presents a good argument that he was not present. See "La Vida de S. Juan de la Cruz," or "El Padre Crisogono de Jesús: Reparos criticos," in *Monte Carmelo* 77 (1969), pp. 8–9.

    2. E. A. Peers, ed., *The Complete Works of St. John of the Cross*, vol. III, (Wheathampstead-Hartfordshire: Anthony Clarke, 1974), p. 297.

    3. BMC, vol. 14, p. 62 (BNM, Ms. 12738, fol. 217).

4. BMC, vol. 14, p. 45 (BNM, Ms. 12738, fol. 184). The same thing is said by Martin de la Asunción, BMC, vol. 14, p. 88 (BNM, Ms. 12738, ca. fol. 132).

5. BMC, vol. 14, p. 28 (BNM, Ms. 12738, ca. fol. 144).

6. *Letter* n. 1, BAC, p. 971 (Kav., p. 736).

7. BMC, vol. 14, p. 384 (BNM, Ms. 19404, ca. fol. 176).

8. BMC, vol. 13, p. 378 (BNM, Ms. 12738, ca. fol. 855).

9. BMC, vol. 13, p. 386 (BNM, Ms. 12738, ca. fol. 559).

10. BNM, 12738, fol. 985.

11. Eulogio de la Virgen del Carmen, *San Juan de la Cruz y sus escritos* (Teología y Siglo XX), (Madrid: Ediciónes Cristiandad, 1969), pp. 246–247.

12. BMC, vol. 14, p. 13 (BNM, Ms. 12738, ca. fol. 127).

Chapter 6

1. *The Living Flame of Love-B* IV, 5, BAC, p. 919 (Kav., p. 710).

2. This painting still exists and can be seen in the monastery in Segovia where one also finds the tomb of Fray Juan de la Cruz.

3. *Letter* n. 26, BAC, pp. 992–993 (Kav., n. 28, p. 761).

4. *Letter* n. 28, BAC, pp. 993–994, (Kav., n. 31, p. 763).

5. BMC, vol. 14, p. 399 (BNM, Ms. 19404, ca. fol. 176).

6. BNM, Ms. 12738, fol. 355.

Epilogue

1. The narration of these events can be found in Alonso de la Madre de Dios, *Vida, virtudes*, fols. 301–340, with further detail and hagiographical additions.

2. For further details and information, see also the fine article by Fr. Tomas de San Juan de la Cruz, "Culto al 'Siervo de Dios' Fray Juan de la Cruz. Historia de unos procesos olvidados" in *Ephemerides Carmeliticae* [Now called *Teresianum*] 4–5 (1950–1954), pp. 13–69. This has been the primary source for my discussion of Fray Juan's beatification and canonization procedures.

3. The renovation work uncovered some surprises. For example, in the entrance, after removing the flooring, they discovered a large Star of David made from bones set into a floor of small rounded stones. Could the monastery which Ana de Peñalosa obtained from another religious community have originally been the home of a Jewish family? Or was it perhaps a synagogue?

4. The Center offers courses and conferences that seek to understand the life and teachings of San Juan de la Cruz as well as Santa Teresa de Avila for today's believers. Moreover, the friars have accommodations for people to stay in the monastery which San Juan built in the sixteenth century for times of reflection, quiet, and retreats. The following website provides more information and the address of the Center: http://personales.mundivia.es/elcarmen/ce_segovia.htm.

5. *The Sayings of Light and Love,* BAC, n. 59, p. 963 (Kav., n. 60, p. 90).

6. *New Oxford Annotated Bible with the Aprocrypha: New Revised Standard Version* (New York: Oxford University Press, 1991).

Appendix A

1. For more insights on how to read John of the Cross, listen to an audio tape of the excellent conference given by Sr. Constance FitzGerald, O.C.D.: "How to Read Teresa and John: Interpretation of Religious Classics" (New York: Alba House Cassettes, 1987).

About the Author

Richard P. Hardy received his doctorate at
the University of Strasbourg, France, and
is a professor of Christian Spirituality,
lecturing in the United States, Canada,
Philippines, and Hong Kong. His workshops, retreats, and conferences on
Carmelite spirituality focus particularly
on St. John of the Cross and St. Teresa of
Avila. He lives in San Francisco.

BOOKS & MEDIA

The Daughters of St. Paul operate book and media centers at the following addresses. Visit, call or write the one nearest you today, or find us on the World Wide Web, www.pauline.org

CALIFORNIA

3908 Sepulveda Blvd, Culver City, CA 90230	310-397-8676
5945 Balboa Avenue, San Diego, CA 92111	858-565-9181
46 Geary Street, San Francisco, CA 94108	415-781-5180

FLORIDA

145 S.W. 107th Avenue, Miami, FL 33174	305-559-6715

HAWAII

1143 Bishop Street, Honolulu, HI 96813	808-521-2731
Neighbor Islands call:	866-521-2731

ILLINOIS

172 North Michigan Avenue, Chicago, IL 60601	312-346-4228

LOUISIANA

4403 Veterans Memorial Blvd, Metairie, LA 70006	504-887-7631

MASSACHUSETTS

885 Providence Hwy, Dedham, MA 02026	781-326-5385

MISSOURI

9804 Watson Road, St. Louis, MO 63126	314-965-3512

NEW JERSEY

561 U.S. Route 1, Wick Plaza, Edison, NJ 08817	732-572-1200

NEW YORK

150 East 52nd Street, New York, NY 10022	212-754-1110
78 Fort Place, Staten Island, NY 10301	718-447-5071

PENNSYLVANIA

9171-A Roosevelt Blvd, Philadelphia, PA 19114	215-676-9494

SOUTH CAROLINA

243 King Street, Charleston, SC 29401	843-577-0175

TENNESSEE

4811 Poplar Avenue, Memphis, TN 38117	901-761-2987

TEXAS

114 Main Plaza, San Antonio, TX 78205	210-224-8101

VIRGINIA

1025 King Street, Alexandria, VA 22314	703-549-3806

CANADA

3022 Dufferin Street, Toronto, ON M6B 3T5	416-781-9131
1155 Yonge Street, Toronto, ON M4T 1W2	416-934-3440